BRITAIN
INVADED

BRITAIN
INVADED

HITLER'S PLANS FOR BRITAIN
A DOCUMENTARY RECONSTRUCTION

ADRIAN GILBERT

C

LONDON SYDNEY AUCKLAND JOHANNESBURG

Published in Great Britain in 1990 by Century

An imprint of Random Century Ltd

20 Vauxhall Bridge Road, London SW1V 2SA

Century Hutchinson Australia (Pty) Ltd

20 Alfred Street, Milsons Point, Sydney, NSW 2061, Australia

Century Hutchinson New Zealand Ltd

PO Box 40-086, 32–34 View Road, Glenfield, Auckland 10,

New Zealand

Century Hutchinson South Africa (Pty) Ltd

PO Box 337, Bergvlei 2012, South Africa

Adrian Gilbert's right to be identified as the author of this work has been asserted by him in accordance with the Copyright, Designs and Patents Act, 1988.

Set in Times Roman and Helvetica.

Art Direction and Book Design by Bob Hook.

Photoset by Rowland Phototypesetting Ltd,

Bury St Edmunds, Suffolk

Printed and bound in Great Britain by

Butler and Tanner Ltd, Frome, Somerset

British Library Cataloguing in Publication data

Gilbert, Adrian

  The last days of Britain: an illustrated history.

  1. Great Britain. Proposed invasion by Germany, 1939–45

  I. Title

  940.5341

  ISBN 0 7126 3909 8

Title page A German Junkers Ju 87 dive bomber in action against British forces, July 1940

C O N T E N T S

PREFACE

The invasion of Great Britain in 1940 was one of the most decisive moments in modern history. Germany's victory – no matter how short-lived – signalled the end of Britain as a major power on the world stage and ushered in a new era where for the next five decades global influence was concentrated in the hands of the two superpowers, the United States of America and the Soviet Union. While many contemporaries regarded Britain's defeat in 1940 as a cruel and unfortunate stroke of fate, removing the nation from its rightful position as a world leader, some later commentators have argued that the war only hastened Britain's inevitable decline from imperial grandeur to the more modest position it holds today.

This book cannot hope to cover such a complex subject as the invasion and occupation of Britain in any great depth. The aim, instead, is to provide the general reader with an illustrated documentary record of Britain in the Second World War.

The many arguments generated by this controversial, and often painful, episode in British history have produced more than their fair share of historiographical mud-slinging. For the record, I would like to point out that all the quotations attributed to named individuals form an accurate record of what was either said or written. The interpretations are, of course, my own.

A book of this nature relies heavily on the past endeavours of many historians (see bibliographical note) but I would also like to acknowledge the help of the following institutions and individuals: the librarian of the Royal United Services Institute, the Imperial War Museum, Howard Cooley, Lionel Leventhal, Donald Somerville, Mandy Little and, most especially, Sally Payne.

Adrian Gilbert, 1990

Right A well-placed stick of German paratroops descends towards the target area alongside Hawkinge airfield, just after dawn on 23 July 1940. The success of airborne operations in the Low Countries ensured the paras were assigned a key role in the invasion plan directed against the United Kingdom.

THE FALL OF FRANCE

1 0 May 1940: the Phoney War ended. At dawn German Stuka dive bombers screamed down on Allied positions, artillery thundered along the front and some 3,000 panzers smashed their way across the border. The German advance heralded a new age of warfare. This was the beginning of Blitzkrieg.

Germany had already been victorious against Poland in 1939, and although the Poles had fought with great bravery their defeat had been inevitable. The true test of strength would lie in Germany's war with France and Great Britain. The Allies, however, had done little since declaring war in September 1939, merely taking up defensive positions along the French border. Having dealt with Poland, the German generals turned their attention to the war in the West. The German plan of attack changed and rechanged during the winter of 1939–40, but finally Operation Sickelstroke emerged, a masterpiece of imaginative thinking that would knock France out of the war in a matter of weeks.

Army Group B (General Fedor von Bock) would advance into Holland and Belgium and eliminate the armed forces of both countries while simul- taneously drawing Franco–British forces into a dangerous position far from the main centre of fighting. The bulk of the German forces in the West – over 45 divisions, including seven panzer and three motorized – were assigned to Army Group A (Colonel-General Gerd von Rundstedt). Deployed at the centre of the German line, the armoured divisions of Army Group A would act as the spearhead of the offensive, driving through the Ardennes, a hilly, wooded region poorly defended by the Allies. Once through the French defences, the panzers would race westward to the Channel, thereby cutting the Allied forces in two.

In marked contrast to the Germans – superbly trained and capably led – the French Army suffered from poor morale and feeble leadership, while the nine divisions of General Lord Gort's British Expeditionary Force (BEF) were too few to be of consequence. The German armed forces put their faith in surprise and mobility. The French, by contrast, trusted in the strength of static defences to blunt offensive action. Imprisoned by the rigidity of their strategic thinking, the French were convinced that the sector opposite the Ardennes would be safe from

Right The humiliation of defeat: British and French troops are led away into captivity after the fall of Dunkirk on 29 May. The complete exhaustion of these men is evident in this photograph, having endured several days of unrelenting bombardment from the guns of German artillery and the dive-bombing Stukas of the Luftwaffe.

Above Generals Ironside and Gort are awarded the Legion of Honour by the French Commander-in-Chief, General Gamelin (far right). The intention of the ceremony was to demonstrate Anglo-French unity, but from the outset of the campaign in the West both armies acted semi-independently.

Above right German paratroopers link up with an infantry unit as they prepare to push on to the Dutch port of Amsterdam. During the fighting in the Low Countries the paras had proved themselves as first-class soldiers; the question remained, how well would they do against Britain?

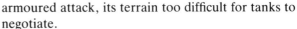

armoured attack, its terrain too difficult for tanks to negotiate.

The German assault in the West caught the Allies unprepared. Army Group B opened the offensive with aerial bombardments and airborne landings against key targets in the Low Countries. Vital airfields and bridges were captured, as German ground forces smashed their way into Holland and Belgium. The Dutch were forced back, flooding their own lands and demolishing strategic obstacles in a vain attempt to stem the German advance. Although the Dutch plan was to fall back on 'Fortress Holland', a heavily fortified area covering Amsterdam and Rotterdam, the speed of the German advance proved too much for their slow-moving troops. Totally overwhelmed, the demoralization of the Dutch was completed by a devastating air raid against Rotterdam on 14 May, an attack which coincided with the decision to surrender – just four days into the German offensive.

In Belgium, the fortress of Eban Emael was taken in one of the most brilliant exploits of the

war. Specially trained airborne troops and assault engineers landed by gliders on the roof of the fortress and rendered it defenceless through the precise application of shaped-charge explosives. As had been the case in 1914, the Belgians' reliance on fixed fortifications did little to impede the German advance. Within days the Belgian Army was retreating in disarray. The German plan was working well, so that Army Group B's success in the Low Countries allowed the armoured divisions of Army Group A to traverse the wooded defiles of the Ardennes without interruption.

Belgian forces put up no measurable opposition to the German panzer divisions as they pushed through the Ardennes before emerging against the main French defensive lines based on the formidable obstacle of the River Meuse. Organized into three panzer corps – XV (Hoth), XXXXI (Reinhardt) and XIX (Guderian) – the first of the German formations reached the east bank of the Meuse on the evening of 12 May.

As each of the three corps prepared to breach the French defences, the most significant attack would be made by Guderian's divisions opposite Sedan. Given the fullest support from the Luftwaffe – whose dive-bombing Stukas, complete with air-driven sirens, struck terror into the French – Guderian's assault infantry crossed the river and secured the high ground on the west bank. French counter-attacks, which might have eliminated the precarious German bridgehead, materialized far too late. Within 24 hours the Germans had consolidated their position and were preparing it as a springboard for the great panzer drive to the Channel coast. Further north, the two corps of Reinhardt and Hoth also crossed the Meuse and without hesitation followed Guderian's lead, pressing on westward. So swift had been the breakthrough that the German tanks had little fighting to do; their role was now to maintain the momentum of the advance despite growing problems of mechanical breakdown and fuel shortages.

The crack 1st and 2nd Panzer Divisions were at

the forefront of the German advance. Tearing across the old battlefields of the First World War, the 1st Panzer Division took Amiens on 20 May. Even more spectacularly, the 2nd Panzer Division captured Abbeville on the same day, advance units reaching the Channel Coast in the evening. In a single week the Germans had achieved their first major objective; the 'panzer corridor' had cut off the French armies (with the BEF) in Belgium and northern France from the main body of the French Army to the south.

During this phase of the fighting the Allies seemed frozen into immobility. When action was taken, it was invariably too little, too late. The Luftwaffe dominated in the air: what existed of the French Air Force was badly deployed and when airborne it failed miserably to prevent the Luftwaffe having a free hand over the battlefield. The RAF pressed home gallant attacks against German targets but with little effect.

On the ground the Allied performance was equally lamentable. Perhaps not surprisingly, Holland and Belgium could do little to stem the German tide, although Belgium's collapse came as a shock. Brussels fell on 17 May and as Army Group B remorselessly drove its way across Belgium so King Leopold and his army found themselves driven out of their country. Leopold's position was becoming steadily more hopeless, and on the night of 27 May he despatched an envoy to the Germans to ask for an immediate ceasefire. Like Holland before her, Belgium was out of the reckoning.

Only France stood any chance of holding the German advance. But the initial disasters on the Meuse and in Belgium would only be compounded by others as the days progressed. General Maurice Gamelin, the French Commander-in-Chief, failed to organize a counter-attack to sever the panzer corridor. The French Army's armoured forces found themselves committed to the battle in small 'penny pockets' that were contained by the German defensive screen with little difficulty.

The inability of the French to come to grips with this disaster expressed itself at the highest level: on the evening of 15 May Gamelin admitted to the French Government that he considered France's position to be hopeless. Shocked by Gamelin's defeatism, the Government replaced him as C-in-C with General Maxime Weygand, a man as old and set in his ways as his 73 years implied. A disastrous choice, Weygand was unacquainted with the situation and too slow-witted to set in motion an appropriate course of action.

The BEF too was taken by surprise at the swiftness of the German offensive, although General Gort assembled an improvised armoured force to counter-attack the panzer corridor. Co-operation with the French south of the corridor was non-existent. Despite this Gort decided that some action must be

Above 'For Who? – For England!' screams this German poster designed to inflame anti-British prejudices amongst the French – later exacerbated by the Royal Navy's attack on the French Fleet.

Below General Heinz Guderian assesses the situation from an armoured car converted to act as a mobile forward HQ. Guderian, along with other panzer commanders, made a special point of advancing with his troops to enable him to make on the spot decisions. Recent developments in communications made this seemingly flamboyant style of command practical: control could be maintained over far-flung forces through the panzer division's sophisticated radio net.

The panzer advance continues: self-propelled artillery (a 4.7cm gun mounted on a PzKpfw I chassis) rolls through a small French town during May 1940.

taken. The attack was launched near Arras on 21 May. The British did well at first, as German troops retreated in disorder, but accurate shooting from heavy anti-tank guns brought the advance to a halt, and the German line was restored.

By now Gort realized that there could be no possibility of turning the tide and the British were forced to withdraw from Arras. The only hope for the BEF and the other Allied troops in Flanders was to retreat north to the Channel ports, make a last-ditch stand and hope that as many men as possible could be evacuated to Britain.

The headlong retreat was a bitter pill for the men of the BEF to swallow, but the panzer divisions of Army Group A snapped relentlessly at the heels of the retreating Allies. Operating on the left of the German line, the three divisions of Guderian's XIX Panzer Corps pushed greedily along the French coast, hoping to capture the three main Channel ports of Boulogne, Calais and Dunkirk and so deprive the Allies of any chance of a successful evacuation. From the east, the formations of Army Group B were pressing hard on a confused mêlée of terrified refugees fighting for road space with a mass of Allied troops. Scenting final victory, the more mobile German divisions began to jockey for position, ready to sweep down in a *coup de grâce*.

The headlong retreat presented a tragic sight: discarded equipment and weapons littered the road side; wounded comrades were left behind to await an uncertain future; gangs of deserters looted their way across the countryside. At the same time, however, there were many instances of heroic self-sacrifice as the rearguard – from all nationalities – fought on to the bitter end.

British reinforcements were sent across the Channel to strengthen the defences of Boulogne and Calais. The garrisons of both ports fought with great determination but in the face of superior numbers, Boulogne fell on 24 May and Calais two days later. Now only Dunkirk remained as an evacuation port for the hard-pressed Allies.

As early as 14 May, Vice Admiral Bertram Ramsay, Flag Officer Dover, had begun to consider the means for a cross-channel evacuation, and the process of collecting suitable craft was instigated. Code-named Operation Dynamo, the rescue of the Allied forces from Dunkirk was put into action late on 26 May. The difficulties faced by the Royal Navy were enormous. The ships were under fire from German artillery on the coast and worse still, they faced

Above The French garrison of Lille surrenders to the Germans during the final stages of the campaign in France. The Germans were so impressed by the French defence around Lille that they accorded their opponents the traditional honours of war, allowing them to march out of the city fully armed and with flags flying.

Right A German photograph of the destruction encountered in Dunkirk: British dead and their vehicles lie scattered across the beach. The British could take some consolation from the knowledge that 62,000 men had been evacuated from Dunkirk, but it could not disguise the fact that the BEF had been destroyed as a fighting force. The losses in men and equipment would become of vital importance in the coming battle for Britain.

constant bombing attacks from the Luftwaffe. Losses of ships were unavoidably high but the Navy (supported in the final phase by volunteer craft crewed by civilians) carried on their work as calmly and efficiently as conditions allowed. On 27 May, 7,669 troops were evacuated. The next day a figure of 17,804 was achieved, using the precarious East Mole and taking men directly off the beaches. On the 29th the figure further improved, rising to 27,310 by late afternoon. The Germans, however, were now perilously close.

On 24 May the panzers of Army Group A had been halted by Hitler with von Rundstedt's approval. Exactly why this order was given will probably never be known but fortunately for the Germans, the order was countermanded that evening following a fierce discussion between Hitler and the Army High Command (OKH). The advance resumed the next day. Any greater delay might well have allowed the bulk of the BEF to escape the German juggernaut.

As the perimeter around Dunkirk began to shrink, so the fighting grew more desperate. The French First Army, encircled around the city of Lille, carried on the battle until forced to surrender on 1 June – a sacrifice that helped the British form a defensive line to cover Dunkirk. But this was to prove only a temporary respite. The collapse of the Belgian Army on 25 May was yet another disaster. Even though Gort had wisely anticipated it, the reinforcements he despatched to cover the threatened sector was insufficient and the Germans drove a wedge through the demoralized Belgians, capturing Nieuport on 27 May and Le Panne the following day. The Allied perimeter was reduced to a 10-mile radius around Dunkirk.

On 29 May the Germans launched a concerted attack on all sides of the perimeter. Short of ammunition and exhausted by days of continuous fighting, the Allied rearguards began to give way. From the west the German panzers hurled themselves at the Allied lines, while on the eastern flank German infantry advanced remorselessly over the sand dunes. The retreating Allied units fell back in confusion to the main evacuation areas. Here the scene was one of pandemonium. The long lines of men waiting to be embarked found themselves under direct artillery fire from the advancing Germans. Some waited in line as the shells rained down on them; others broke and ran, either to the comparative safety of the dunes or to their deaths as they attempted in vain to reach the evacuation boats.

At 5.45 pm the British Commander-in-Chief, Lieutenant-General Harold Alexander (Gort had been reluctantly ordered out the previous day), accepted that the position was hopeless. He radioed to the Navy to cease the embarkation and withdraw to safety while he despatched a staff officer to negotiate a surrender. As the first German panzers reached the beaches they received the order that the British had surrendered and fighting was to cease forthwith. The Germans stood on their tanks to watch the extraordinary sight of long columns of British and French troops wending their way past them into captivity.

Vice Admiral Ramsay had originally considered an evacuation figure of 45,000 to be reasonable, so the removal of over 62,000 men (including 10,000 French) from Dunkirk represented a minor triumph. Yet the very fact that over 150,000 of the best troops in the British Army had been captured at Dunkirk was a desperate blow. Not only that, the soldiers who had escaped brought with them little more than their rifles – the rest of their arms and equipment lay scattered over northern France. The losses included 2,472 guns, 63,879 vehicles and 500,000 tons of vital military supplies.

Following the surrender at Dunkirk, the Germans prepared to crush the remains of the French Army, now holding a defensive line along the River Somme. Although the French fought with more resolution than before, they could do little to stop the German advance. A series of adroitly co-ordinated attacks were launched on 5 June and once the panzers had broken through the enemy defences they raced across France. German progress was dictated only by the endurance and speed of their vehicles. On 14 June, Paris was abandoned to the Germans; just three days later the French, under a new government led by Marshal Pétain, asked for an armistice which came into effect on 22 June. Northern France and the western seaboard came under direct German control. The remainder of the country was to be ruled by the collaborationist Pétain government from the old spa town of Vichy.

During this last phase of the campaign in France, Hitler had not forgotten his enemy across the Channel. Throughout June the German General Staff had been busy with additional work, drawing up plans to defeat Britain once and for all – by seaborne invasion.

Above German infantry march under the Arc de Triomphe as part of the victory celebrations following the surrender of France on 22 June. In just six weeks the Wehrmacht had destroyed the French Army and the BEF. Now anything seemed possible to the German High Command — even an invasion of England.

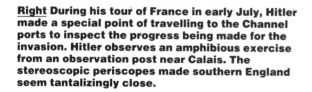

Right During his tour of France in early July, Hitler made a special point of travelling to the Channel ports to inspect the progress being made for the invasion. Hitler observes an amphibious exercise from an observation post near Calais. The stereoscopic periscopes made southern England seem tantalizingly close.

THE GERMAN PLAN

Ironically, Admiral Erich Raeder's meeting with Hitler on 21 May 1940 marked the true genesis of the plan to invade Britain. Yet the private conference had not gone as Raeder intended. As Commander-in-Chief of the Kriegsmarine (German Navy), Raeder was fearful of his forces being involved in Hitler's highly dangerous expansionist foreign policies. His Navy had still not recovered from the campaign in Norway during April 1940 and Raeder had hoped to forestall any prospect of an attack on Britain. To Raeder's consternation, however, Hitler seized upon the idea of an invasion and informed him that if the German peace terms were rejected then an assault would almost certainly follow.

Hitler's primary concern was still with the campaign in France, but he reasoned that the occupation of the French coast made an invasion of Britain a strong possibility. Earlier plans drawn up in 1939 – for an assault across the North Sea from German ports – had never been seriously considered, but this sudden change in Germany's fortunes transformed the strategic situation.

After the Allied disaster at Dunkirk, with the defeat of France only a formality, the staff officers of the German armed forces High Command (OKW) began to draw up the invasion plans. Bernhard von Lossberg was a lieutenant-colonel on OKW's planning section, and his comment sums up the feelings of the German Army at the time:

> 'As our troops stood around Calais after the victory . . . they saw before them the chalk cliffs of Dover on the other side of the Channel. In the exaltation of past success these German soldiers and their leaders came to believe themselves capable of things that no one even dared think of before the West Offensive. Thus . . . the thought was born to land in England.'

In this new mood of confidence, representatives from the three armed services began to meet regularly to discuss the many problems that such a plan would inevitably throw up.

As the premier service within the German armed forces, the Army took the initiative, but their plans almost immediately foundered on the rocks of reasonable Navy objections. The German Navy was only too aware of the difficulties of an amphibious operation against a nation with powerful air and

Right The German Chancellor addresses the Reichstag in packed session. In these meetings German policy decisions were outlined to the world at large, and during June 1940 included appeals to Britain to give up the struggle. Hitler would have preferred not to invade, but the defiant refusal of the Churchill government to come to terms led the Germans to look towards a direct military solution.

naval forces. Initially the Army showed little appreciation of the scale of the enterprise. At the first major inter-service conference, General Jodl, OKW's Chief-of-Staff, had blithely set down the Army's approach to the vexed question of getting the troops across the Channel:

> 'The landing must therefore be effected in the form of a mighty river-crossing on a broad front, where the air force takes the role of artillery; the first wave of crossing forces must be very strong, and . . . bridge building will be replaced by the creation of a sea transport road, completely secure against attack from the sea, in the Dover Narrows.'

Three armies were assigned for the invasion – Sixteenth, Ninth and Sixth – deployed east to west from Belgium to the Cherbourg Peninsula in Normandy. They intended to launch a broad front crossing from Ramsgate, in the easternmost part of Kent, along 200 miles of coast to Lyme Bay in Dorset. The main thrust of the attack would be made in south-east England. Once sufficient forces were ashore, German armoured units would spearhead a general advance, swinging around London northward to take up a line from the River Severn to Maldon in Essex.

The German Navy's role was two-fold: firstly, to ferry the ground forces and their supplies across the Channel and secondly, to protect the amphibious forces from attack by the Royal Navy. The Kriegsmarine, however, lacked the resources to fulfil either role adequately: there were insufficient transports to trans-ship the forces deemed necessary by the Army, and the Royal Navy not only outnumbered the Kriegsmarine in every class of vessel, its fighting reputation was second to none.

Throughout June, the Navy and Army planners argued their respective points of view. Something

Left Hitler meets his three service chiefs: Marshal Hermann Göring (Air Force), General Walther von Brauchitsch (Army) and Admiral Erich Raeder (Navy). Although the Wehrmacht (armed forces) was plagued by disputes between the three services, it worked well enough during the early years of the war. The preparations for the invasion of Britain would call for a high level of inter-service co-operation, and stretch the planners to the limit.

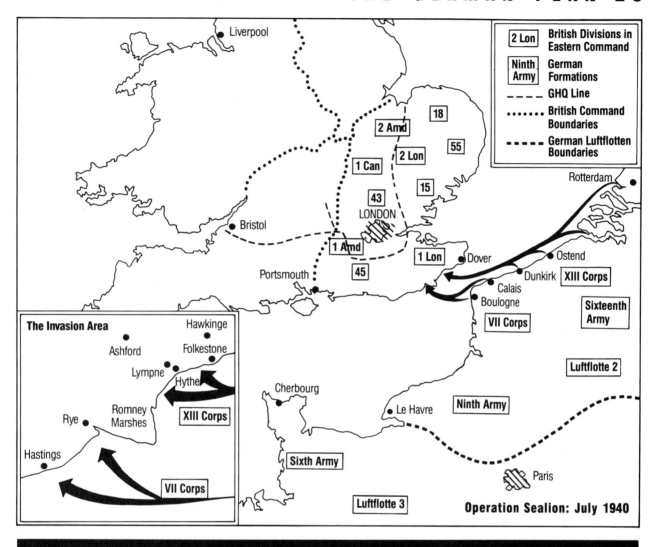

The Invasion Area

Operation Sealion: July 1940

Legend:
- 2 Lon — British Divisions in Eastern Command
- Ninth Army — German Formations
- — — — GHQ Line
- ········· British Command Boundaries
- – – – German Luftflotten Boundaries

had to give. Bit by bit the Army's grandiose plans were trimmed, firstly from a three-army assault to two and finally to an attack by the Sixteenth Army alone – on a narrow frontage from Folkestone to Hastings. The Army had protested bitterly that this would prevent adequate deployment of their panzer divisions – the key to Blitzkrieg strategy – but the Navy was adamant, and in this they had an ally in the Air Force.

Reichsmarshall Hermann Göring was no friend of the Kriegsmarine. In the past he had repeatedly boasted that the Luftwaffe would replace the need for a navy. On this occasion, however, he supported the recommendations of his own staff who concluded

Above A photograph of one of the invasion ports taken by an RAF reconnaissance aircraft, 24 June 1940. The areas within the white dotted lines reveal the presence of various German invasion craft, whose numbers were to increase further as the days progressed.

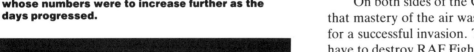

that aerial support for the wide-fronted Army plan would not be feasible given the enormous demands expected of them.

On both sides of the Channel it was appreciated that mastery of the air was the essential prerequisite for a successful invasion. Thus, the Luftwaffe would have to destroy RAF Fighter Command in the initial phase of the campaign. Then, once the invasion was underway, it would be required to act as aerial artillery for the amphibious forces during the critical first few days of the landings. It would also have to prevent the movement of British forces attempting

**Below The Luftwaffe contribution to the invasion
fleet: Siebel craft. Driven by powerful aircraft
engines they were constructed from engineer river
pontoons in catamaran fashion and were capable
of speeds of around nine knots. Although they could
carry up to 60 tons of stores they were mainly
used as floating gun platforms.**

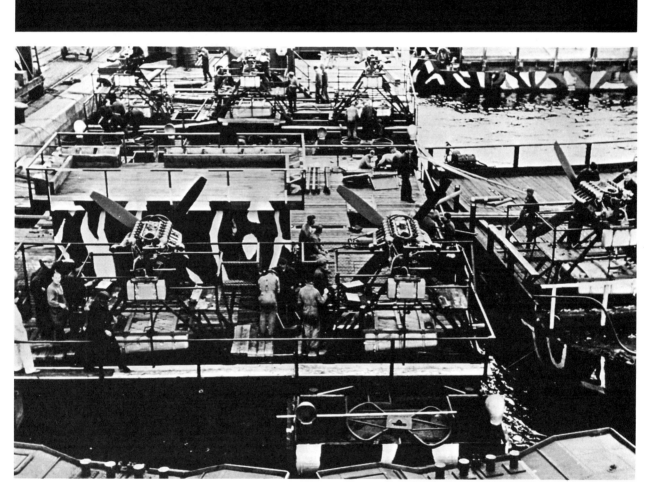

to counter-attack the German beach-head. Lastly, the Luftwaffe would be called upon to support the Kriegsmarine in holding open the invasion route against the onslaught from the Royal Navy.

On the diplomatic front Hitler sent out peace feelers to Britain which, if only in the dictator's mind, were models of statesmanlike generosity. While a substantial element of the British establishment was for coming to terms with Germany – especially after France's decision to sue for peace – the British Prime Minister, Winston Churchill, was resolutely defiant. He made it clear that no more accommodations would be made with Nazi Germany and the war would go on until victory or defeat. Enraged by these rebuffs, most notably the scornful rejection of his 'Last Appeal to Reason' speech, Hitler determined to invade. The question simply remained, when?

All three members of the Wehrmacht invasion committee agreed that swiftness and success were inextricably linked. The more time the British had to lick their wounds and reorganize their shattered Army, the more capable they would be of resisting invasion. Colonel Heinrich von Stülpnagel, the Army representative, argued that this was a unique moment in the course of the war: '. . . never has England been so weak; if we do not invade with the greatest alacrity, then history's verdict will be hard to answer'.

The Army claimed it would be ready by early July and from the first days of June the Luftwaffe was busy preparing its forward airfields in northern France and Belgium for the coming aerial battle. As ever the Navy's requirements were paramount but more difficult to fulfil. They were based on the dictates of a suitable high tide for a dawn landing – a fact not much understood by the Army until staff cars parked on the beach began to disappear under incoming tides – and enough time to improvise an invasion fleet. The Navy considered it would have sufficient vessels ready for a four-division landing by the end of the first week of July. Allowing for appropriate tides and a degree of moonlight, 13 July was chosen as S-Day, although, as later events were to show, this would have to be revised forward.

Somewhat sceptical of the outcome, the Navy nevertheless set about fulfilling its tasks in a professional manner. Effective control of the naval side of Operation Sea Lion – the code name for the invasion – was assigned to the Fleet Commander, Vice-Admiral Lütjens. He was ably supported by Commodore Ruge who was also responsible for the clearing and re-clearing of British mines while setting up protective German mine barriers on the flanks of the invasion route.

During June, Germany and western Europe were scoured for suitable landing craft for despatch to the main invasion ports: Rotterdam, Antwerp, Ostend, Dunkirk, Calais, Boulogne, Le Havre. All energies were devoted to assembling the fleet, not only along the coast but further inland. The historian Walter Ansel wrote: 'The invasion complex had settled to a zone stretching from Rotterdam to Le Havre along the sea, and inland from Koblenz to Paris.'

The work-horse of the invasion fleet was the prahm, a canal or river barge ranging in size from

Right German sailors prepare some of the many prahms for the amphibious invasion. Barges normally employed in negotiating Europe's waterways, prahms were far from ideal vessels for the Channel crossing but they were at least readily available and needed only limited conversion to this new role.

two to seven hundred tons. Hurriedly converted to act as the beach assault craft, it could carry troops, weapons and equipment. Alongside the 2,000 or more prahms commandeered by the Navy were a wide assortment of coastal craft including tugs, steamers, trawlers, motor coasters, motor boats and storm boats (*Sturmboote*). This latter type of vessel was a fast combat-engineer launch, small enough to be carried on trawlers and minesweepers. Once close to the shore it would be launched from the parent vessel, depositing small assault squads of six to eight men on to the beach before returning for further squads. Other specialist craft included motor coasters armed with field guns to provide some artillery support for the infantry, essentially to encourage morale after exercises revealed the shortcomings in accuracy of fire from even the most gently pitching vessel.

The four divisions selected from Colonel-General Ernst Busch's Sixteenth Army to form the First Wave of the invasion were organized into VII Corps (1st Mountain and 7th Infantry Divisions) on the left flank and XIII Corps (35th and 17th Infantry Divisions) on the right. The VII Corps, sailing from Boulogne and Calais, would land on C Beach (Hastings to Lydd) and XIII Corps, sailing from Ostend, Dunkirk and Rotterdam, was assigned to B Beach (New Romney to Folkestone). The First Wave was divided into three echelons – all told, taking two or even three days to land – and once on shore constituted a force of 110,000 men and nearly 25,000 horses (the German Army still relied heavily on horse-drawn transport in 1940).

The basic unit within the invasion fleet was a tug or trawler which would tow two prahms in tandem. Six of these made up a tow group capable of transporting a reinforced battalion. The tow groups were instructed to keep formation during the Channel crossing before making the final dash to the shore. Elaborate plans were drawn up but few of the naval commanders had much faith in anything above 'semi-organized chaos'. Ruge summed it up best

Right The German Navy puts the invasion fleet through its paces. In this instance a tug can be seen towing two converted prahms – the basic amphibious unit. Six of these would form a tow group, capable of transporting a reinforced battalion of anything up to a 1,000-men strong.

when he said: '. . . [we had] to get them, the prahms and other landing craft, all out of port and then make one agreed-upon signal, "Formation Pigpile (*Sauhaufen*). Go to England!"' In other words it was accepted that the convoy plans might swiftly break down, the invasion fleet reduced to a herd that the Navy could only guide to the other shore as best they could.

The First Wave divisions were ordered to gain their respective beach-heads before pushing inland to secure a defensive line capable of withstanding counter-attack. The most difficult task of this first phase was assigned to the veteran troops of 17th Infantry Division on the right of the German line. Fortunately, they would receive help from the Luftwaffe in the form of the 7th Air Division – victors of the airborne operations in the Low Countries – who were to be parachuted *en masse* just to the north of Folkestone and Hythe in order to capture the two strategic airfields of Hawkinge and Lympne.

Once this had been completed, the paratroopers would join up with the 17th Division to march eastward with the utmost speed to take Dover from the rear – its vital port facilities were considered essential to subsequent phases of the German plan. With Dover secure, advance elements of the two division were to dash along the London Road to Canterbury and prepare a defensive line northward to the coast and south-west towards Ashford. The 35th Infantry Division, to the immediate left of the 17th Division, would be landed on the shelving beaches alongside Dynmouth, its job to push inland to capture the heights above Romney Marshes and then advance to defensive positions near Ashford.

Further west, the other side of Dungeness, were the two divisions of VII Corps: 7th Infantry Division would land on the beaches by Camber and Rye Harbour ready to secure the western half of Romney Marshes and the two Cinque ports of Rye and Winchelsea; 1st Mountain Division was to be brought ashore facing the cliffs and rocky coves either side of Fairlight in order to advance north-west, capturing Hastings and Bexhill before digging in to secure the left flank of the beach-head.

Once dug in, the First Wave would be buttressed by the arrival of the 22nd Air Landing Division – assuming the airfields were in German hands – but they were told not to expect seaborne reinforcement for anything up to eight or ten days. During this critical time they would have to weather the storm of the British counter-attack on their own.

Fully aware of the gravity of the task, General Busch's troops trained themselves relentlessly in the new but complex art of amphibious warfare. If at the highest level German Army–Navy relations remained traditionally poor, they developed with surprising rapidity at field command level. Not only did Busch and Lütjens regularly meet to discuss progress but a number of other experts made valuable contributions. Among these was General Georg Hans Reinhardt, the commander of the XXXXI Panzer Corps during the recent victorious campaign in France and now the Army's expert on amphibious armour operations. Working with the greatest zeal on the training grounds at Putlos and Sylt, Reinhardt developed a number of U (*Unterwasser*) tanks, capable of travelling underwater for short periods. These tanks were to be deployed with conventionally 'proofed' amphibious tanks to provide an armoured punch for the infantry divisions of the First Wave.

The High Command of the German Army was confident that if the First Wave divisions got ashore and hung on for the Second Wave formations (with their substantial panzer element), they would have no serious problems in overwhelming the British Army – or what was left of it. German intelligence of the British Army's Order of Battle was broadly accurate. If the Germans could put sufficient numbers of men and weapons ashore, then Britain's defeat would be an almost foregone conclusion. By early July a quiet confidence was discernible on the German side of the Channel, a mood not shared by their opponents on the other side.

Above right Even though the Germans were unused to the complexities of amphibious operations they took every opportunity to train their troops in the details of this new form of warfare. Here infantry prepare to embark on a troopship in Ostend.

Right General Georg Hans Reinhardt (left) talks to one of his divisional commanders. Not only had Reinhardt developed amphibious tanks for the armoured units, he would later play a key role in the panzer breakout through southern England.

BRITAIN AT BAY

he disaster at Dunkirk came as a profound shock to the British people. Despite the fact that substantial numbers of British and Allied troops filtered back to Britain from other French ports, the British Expeditionary Force had been soundly defeated. This was Britain's greatest military defeat since Cornwallis's surrender at Yorktown during the American War of Independence. Most people were quick to realize that the fall of France left Britain dangerously isolated.

The level of German activity along the northern French coastline was an obvious indicator of their possible intentions; the problem for British intelligence was to discover exactly where and when? Aerial reconnaissance revealed the build-up of large numbers of naval craft in Channel ports by the end of June but this gave no indication of their intended destination – would it be the south coast or (as most thought) East Anglia? Only when the German fleet had put to sea would the British know that the invasion was on. The British planners were forced to play a waiting game, while desperately attempting to improvise a defensive system.

The British Chiefs-of-Staff were unanimous in their agreement that the air defence of the island was critical to Britain's survival. If the RAF lost control of its own skies then German troops could make virtually unmolested landings along Britain's coastline. Equally serious, the Royal Navy would find itself in a cripplingly vulnerable position in Britain's coastal waters, unable to operate effectively in the face of the Luftwaffe's enormous bombing capacity. Every effort was made to bring Britain's air defences up to strength, but it was a race against time.

While the RAF prepared, the Royal Navy was suddenly faced with a formidable crisis. The Italian declaration of war on 10 June was followed in succession by the French surrender. The loss of the powerful French Fleet was a dreadful blow to the British in the Mediterranean, while almost overnight the Italian Fleet had become a serious and direct threat to Britain's vital trade artery to the East. Despite the grim situation, a substantial battle group (Force H) was sent to Gibraltar in order to hold Britain's sea lanes open through the Mediterranean.

The Italian Fleet could be contained by an aggressive British presence but the French position remained a major worry, especially as it seemed

Right One of the many posters and leaflets issued by the British Government in the summer of 1940. Although useful in preparing the civilian population for the coming invasion they were no substitute for a large, well-equipped and fully trained force capable of destroying the German Army on the beaches.

ENEMY INVASION.

WHAT YOU MUST DO.

Remain at work : when unable to do so and you have no invasion duty

CONTACT YOUR LOCAL WARDEN.

He will arrange for you to help the City to carry on.

If you are in Civil Defence, that is your job.

If you have no invasion duty, stand firm.

Do not leave your district ; do not block the roads.

Do not listen to rumours ; only obey orders given by the military, police, Civil Defence personnel or Ministry of Information.

Be on your guard against Fifth Columnists.

Apply to your local Warden for more detailed instructions.

possible that Marshal Pétain's new Vichy Government might hand over French battleships and cruisers to German control. When the French Navy refused the British request for the ships to be either disarmed or removed from Vichy influence, the Royal Navy decided to take action. Although the French vessels in Alexandria Harbour surrendered, no such agreement was reached with the main French force at Mers-el-Kebir in Algeria. On 3 July the battleships of Force H attacked their former ally in a doleful encounter that removed any potential threat to Britain in the Mediterranean but caused a severe deterioration of Franco–British relations.

Besides these special problems in the Mediterranean, the Royal Navy had worldwide commitments which acted as a further drain on resources for the defence of the United Kingdom. Despite this, the Home Fleet could still deploy forces considerably more powerful than anything fielded by the German Kriegsmarine. The capital ships *Nelson*, *Rodney*, *Valiant*, *Renown*, *Repulse* and *Barham* of the Main Fleet at Scapa Flow were supported by cruiser and destroyer flotillas from the regional commands of Rosyth, Nore, Dover, Portsmouth and Western Approaches.

If the barriers of the RAF and the Royal Navy were breached, then the British Army would be called upon to act as the next and final line of defence. To an island people who had not suffered the agonies of invasion and occupation, the defence of Britain had always seemed merely theoretical and ranked low in the Army's list of priorities. After Dunkirk it began to take on a new, painful reality. As Commander-in-Chief of Britain's Home Forces, General Sir Edmund Ironside was forced to review the existing defence plans.

In addition to the men who had escaped from Dunkirk, approximately 100,000 British soldiers managed to get out from other French ports before the arrival of the Germans, but invariably with little more than the weapons they carried. As trained soldiers they were invaluable but it would take weeks to reorganize and re-equip them. For the time being Ironside would have to rely on the existing divisions in Britain.

In the immediate aftermath of Dunkirk, Ironside had at his disposal 15 infantry divisions (most drastically understrength) plus most of the 1st Armoured Division and a still incomplete and partially trained 2nd Armoured Division. Some divisions could only muster half their establishment strength of 15,500

men. Worse still was the desperate shortage of weapons, especially artillery, most of which were old 18-pounders and 4.5-inch howitzers from the previous war.

Equally serious were the shortages of armoured fighting vehicles: most of the Army's best tanks were now on the wrong side of the Channel, in German hands. On 1 June 1940 the only effective AFVs available to General Ironside were 103 Cruiser and

Top The three British service chiefs: General Sir Edmund Ironside, Air Chief Marshal Sir Cyril Newall and Admiral Sir Dudley Pound.
Above An example of the desperate state of British defences, a dummy aircraft intended to fool German aerial reconnaissance.
Above right French capital ships ablaze following the British bombardment at Mers-el-Kebir.
Right Polish troops march through a British town in early July, one of the many foreign units serving in Britain during this period.

110 Infantry tanks, a pitiful number to expect to crush the German beach-head and stem the panzer Blitzkrieg. In considering the overall situation the Chiefs-of-Staff were forced to admit: '. . . should the Germans succeed in establishing a force with its vehicles in this country, our army forces have not got the offensive power to drive it out.'

For the purposes of defence, Britain was divided into a series of Army Commands: Scotland, Western, Northern, Southern and Eastern – the latter covering the critical areas of East Anglia, the home counties and the south coast from Kent to Portsmouth. In the Official History, *The Defence of Britain*, Basil Collier summed up the desperate position of the formations in this area:

'In Eastern Command, whose troops would take the first shock of a seaborne landing anywhere within those limits, there were six divisions with less than half their approved establishment of field guns and with only a handful of anti-tank guns . . . The vital sector from Sheppey to Rye was manned by 1st London Division with 23 field guns towards an establishment of 72, no anti-tank guns, no armoured cars, no armoured fighting vehicles, and about one sixth of the anti-tank rifles to which it was entitled.'

Four divisions (18th, 2nd London, 55th, 15th) were deployed in East Anglia while just two divisions were stationed along the south coast (1st London and 45th). GHQ held the 1st Canadian, 43rd and 52nd Infantry Divisions and the two armoured divisions in central reserve, but as the nearest of these was over 100 miles from the actual invasion area in Kent they could do little to forestall a landing. Indeed, the very idea of a counter-attacking reserve force was nullified by the Army's lack of mobility. While the Army used its own trucks for the transport of supplies, it was forced to commandeer whatever civilian motor coaches it could for the troops; otherwise it was a case of the infantry being reduced to the traditional role of 'footslogger'.

Ironside's aim was to 'prevent the enemy from running riot and tearing the guts out of the country as had happened in France and Belgium', but his forces' lack of weapons, equipment, mobility and general training was a severe handicap. During June and July Ironside and his staff attempted to develop a plan that combined a number of mobile (or semi-mobile) columns with static defences along the coast

and inland. At the heart of the system was the GHQ Line, a series of linked anti-tank obstacles covering London and the Midlands, augmented by a number of 'stop lines' sited between the GHQ Line and the coastal defences.

As early as 14 May, Anthony Eden had called for volunteers from men of military age not actually in the armed services. The response was overwhelming, as tens of thousands of men from all walks of life offered their services in this hour of need. Organized on a regional basis, the Home Guard, as it was called, quickly spread across the country. Training was rudimentary and not much was expected of the Home Guard but its potential effectiveness was severely compromised by the dearth of suitable weapons and equipment. Even as late as mid-July, less than half of Home Guard units had been equipped with the appropriate smallarms, the remainder having to make do with shotguns or old sporting rifles. In some cases they were reduced to fielding a variety of edged weapons, pitch forks and cudgels.

While the platoons of the Home Guard were drilled into some form of military efficiency, an army of over 150,000 civilians laboured across southern England, building defensive works and constructing obstacles. Concrete and brick pill-boxes sprang up across the country; coastal resorts were surrounded by coils of barbed wire, the seafronts transformed by sandbag emplacements and the beaches mined. Sadly, however, this work was rarely of military value.

The desire to 'do something' swept across the nation and the War Office was inundated with offers of help from a variety of 'experts' – the majority highly dubious. One such scheme given official backing came under the heading of chemical warfare and involved spraying the sea in coastal areas with a petroleum solution. If an invasion was attempted the sea was to be 'set on fire' and the Germans consumed in the conflagration. In the event, the invaders failed to provide sufficient warning for the scheme to be put into operation.

By the middle of July the Army's position had improved slightly. The arrival of reinforcements now meant that the infantry divisions were getting back to establishment strength, although shortages in artillery and tanks remained as fundamental as ever. During this period Ironside's defensive plans began to come under increasing attack from the Chiefs-of-Staff. They noted that '. . . the balance of the defence

<u>Above</u> A British soldier surveys the barbed-wire defences along the beach at Sandgate between Hythe and Folkestone, 10 July 1940. Two weeks later this stretch of coastline would be the scene of the attack by the German 17th Infantry Division.

<u>Right</u> A frontal view of the 6-inch guns defending Shoeburyness, 26 June 1940. For the most part defences such as these were bypassed by the invading forces.

leant too far on the side of a thinly held crust on the coast, with insufficient reserves in immediate proximity to points where penetration might be expected.'

Confidence in Ironside began to wane and it was suggested that he should be replaced by a younger man. On 20 July, Ironside stood down in place of General Sir Alan Brooke who commenced the process of reorganizing Britain's defences. The timing

Above As the threat of invasion drew nearer the British people took consolation in ridiculing the enemy. Radio, West-End theatres and the music halls resounded to the laughter of audiences confronted by caricatures of 'That Man', ranging from those of Tommy Handley to the one pictured here.

Right Complete with medal ribbons from the first war, this veteran Home Guardsman is seen off on evening patrol. He is armed with an early model Thompson sub-machine gun, fitted with the 50-round drum magazine much favoured by American gangsters during the prohibition period.

of the change-over was perhaps unfortunate in retrospect. Brooke only had a few days before the Germans did land in Kent. In the ensuing post mortems the disruption caused by the change of command was cited by some as an important factor in the British defeat.

During June and July 1940 the military aspects of British life loomed large but it was also a time of intense diplomatic activity. While much of the world was sympathetic to Britain's plight, only the United States of America was in any position to provide practical help. President Roosevelt, a staunch opponent of Nazism, was constrained by his country's firm commitment to neutrality. Only outright German aggression could have brought America into the war and, in this period at least, Germany was careful to avoid any such confrontation. Roosevelt reluctantly had to tell his friend Churchill that Britain would be on its own in the coming battle.

Unfortunately for Britain, the US Ambassador in London, Joe Kennedy, was certainly no Anglophile and he had little faith in the country's prospects for the coming battle. Much to Churchill's discomfiture, Kennedy enthusiastically broadcast his opinions to the world at large. The Ambassador was reported to have told an assembly of neutral journalists that he expected Hitler to be striding down Whitehall by the middle of August. The Foreign Office retort was that 'He is the biggest Fifth Columnist in the country'. Kennedy was something of an exception as most Americans were favourably disposed to the British cause, but along with the other neutrals few gave Britain more than a sporting chance.

The vast majority of the British people were solidly behind Churchill's uncompromising stand against Germany but certain powerful elements within the establishment did not share the popular enthusiasm for the fight and would have preferred a negotiated peace with Hitler. They felt the war had been forced upon Britain by warmongers and that Britain would be better off allied with Germany and fighting the 'common foe of Bolshevism'. Aware of this, the German security services worked carefully to develop contacts and exploit the situation to their advantage.

A special target of German interest was the Duke of Windsor who, since his abdication in 1936, had been living in the South of France. Vain and weak, the Duke was a fervent supporter of Nazi Germany, and his public pronouncements in favour of the Hitler regime were a constant embarrassment to the British Government. On a visit to the Reich before hostilities had begun, he had spoken wildly of Hitler's achievement: 'It cannot be grasped, and is a miracle; one can only begin to understand it when one realizes that behind it all is one man and one will.' After the fall of France the Windsors left for Spain where they were fêted by leading Spanish fascists and pro-German sympathizers.

Once the decision had been made to invade Britain, the German Foreign Office and security services set about winning the Duke of Windsor's support for the scheme. In return the playboy Duke would be offered large sums of cash and a chance to play a suitably regal role in a post-war Britain.

The Duke of Windsor moved to Portugal, ready to sail to the Bahamas after ostensibly accepting the British Government's offer of the Governership of the Crown Territory. During July a series of German agents and emissaries were sent to the Iberian Peninsula to persuade the Duke to accept a 'better offer'. Typically he wavered until the arrival of no less a person than the Führer's deputy Rudolf Hess tipped the balance. The Duke was secretly brought back to Spain to discuss in detail Hess's (wholly specious) 'Seven-Point Peace Plan'. The Duke of Windsor, ever receptive to flattery, was carefully encouraged to see himself in the role of peacemaker between the two nations. The Germans, however, considered him nothing more than a useful propaganda tool, and should he prove amenable, a puppet ruler for the future.

Above The Duke and Duchess of Windsor meet Hitler at Berchtesgaden shortly before the outbreak of war. Edward remained a devoted admirer of the Führer throughout his life.

Right The Windsors are taken on an official tour of a model German housing development during their visit of 1937.

Left Senior British officers meet to discuss forthcoming strategy, from left to right: Lord Gort and his two former corps commanders, Generals Sir John Dill and Sir Alan Brooke. The BEF's failure in France and Belgium marked the end of Gort's career as a serving general.

THE AIR BATTLE OVER BRITAIN

Of all the three sevices within the Wehrmacht, the Luftwaffe was expected to open the offensive against Britain. Although Göring boasted that he would crush the RAF in a few days, his subordinates adopted more sober estimates. Fortunately for the Germans, the Luftwaffe was at the height of its powers in the summer of 1940, and plans for the aerial subjugation of Britain proceeded with surprising rapidity.

Field Marshal Albert Kesselring's Luftflotte (Air Fleet) 2 was deployed along the Channel coast while Field Marshal Hugo Sperrle's Luftflotte 3 attended to the destruction of the French Army, before being redeployed to support Kesselring in north-west France. In Norway – now under German control – General Hans-Jürgen Stumpff's Luftflotte 5 was being assembled to launch feint attacks against northern England and Scotland, thus preventing the RAF from concentrating its forces in southern England.

The German plan was to destroy RAF Fighter Command (so that the Luftwaffe could roam at will over south-east England) and, if possible, to cripple RAF Bomber Command's offensive capability. Once aerial supremacy was gained, the Luftwaffe could concentrate on providing support for the German Army by attacking enemy ground forces and preventing the Royal Navy from cutting through the supply lifeline from Continent to beach-head.

Each Luftflotte was a self-contained entity that included all the various types of aircraft used by the Germans in 1940. The central core of the Fleet was the bomber force, which consisted of Dornier Do 17s, Heinkel He 111s and Junker Ju 88s. All were medium bombers which, as the coming battle proved, relied heavily on fighter protection. Working alongside the bombers was the Junkers Ju 87, a single-engined dive bomber (better known as the Stuka) which was highly vulnerable against the latest fighters but a superb precision bombing tool in experienced hands.

Protecting the bombers were two types of fighter, the Messerschmitt Bf 110 and the Messerschmitt Bf 109. The Bf 110 was a twin-engined long-range escort and although powerfully armed, it compared poorly as a fighter against the single-engined Bf 109. One of the great fighters of the Second World War, the Bf 109's performance was broadly similar to that of the British Spitfire.

In contrast to the German Luftflotten system, the RAF was organized into separate Commands

Right A member of the Observer Corps stands on a roof top in central London, peering through his binoculars for the sight of a German aircraft. St Paul's Cathedral dominates the skyline in the background. The British expected the main weight of the attack to fall upon the capital but as the aerial battle developed the Luftwaffe turned instead to the bombing of Fighter Command airfields.

Above Field Marshal Albert Kesselring (right)
discusses progress with his airmen of Luftflotte 2
during the initial stages of the air attack. A former
artillery officer, Kesselring was considered by
many to be the ablest commander within the
Luftwaffe. His nickname of 'Smiling Albert' is
borne out in this photograph.

based on aircraft type and role. Fighter Command
was the key to the British defensive system, although
Bomber Command became increasingly important
as the invasion developed. The Spitfire was a superb
fighter aircraft and alongside the Hurricane (slower
and slightly less manoeuvrable) it was the backbone
of Fighter Command.

Britain's aerial defence also relied on the early
warning system based on radio detection or Radar.
Operating in conjunction with Radar was the Observer Corps who provided visual plots of enemy
aircraft once they were over Britain. Radar was well
known to the Germans in 1940 but they had not yet
used this device to detect the presence and movement
of aircraft at long range. Once the air battle began
in earnest, however, General Martini, the Luftwaffe
Chief of Signals, began to take a growing interest in
the new invention.

Under the leadership of Air Chief Marshal Sir
Hugh Dowding, Fighter Command was divided into
a series of Groups covering the United Kingdom.
Number 11 Group would bear the brunt of the German attack and was the best defended. The RAF
entered the battle at a severe disadvantage: in
early July its single-seat fighters numbered around
500. The Luftwaffe's strength was significantly,
if not overwhelmingly, superior: over 800 Bf 109s,
250 Bf 110s, over 300 Ju 87 dive bombers and
nearly 1,200 bombers. The Luftwaffe was also employing a significant number of reconnaissance
aircraft for mine-laying duties. While the bulk of
German mines was sown by conventional maritime
means, the Luftwaffe was able to place small numbers

of mines in key areas with speed and accuracy.

The RAF was also at a disadvantage in terms of personnel. Even though most Fighter Command pilots were good fliers they lacked the combat skills of their German counterparts who had fought over Poland and France. RAF tactical doctrine lagged significantly behind that of the Luftwaffe; for example, the German fighter pilots flew in a *Schwarm* or 'finger-four' formation while the men of Fighter Command had been taught to fly the rigid and tactically inferior 'Vic-3' system. The top German aces readily acknowledged the quality of British equipment and the bravery of RAF pilots, but thought little of the 'Hendon flying show' stunts.

The new British Minister for Aircraft Production, Lord Beaverbrook, did his best to increase the production and supply of fighter aircraft, but the shortage of trained pilots remained critical: there was simply not enough time to train pilots to handle

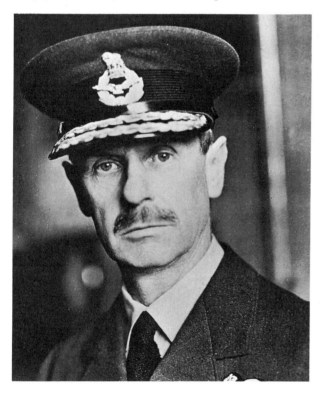

Above An official photograph of Air Chief Marshal Sir Hugh Dowding, who led Fighter Command in its desperate battle against the Luftwaffe for aerial mastery over southern England.

high-speed fighter aircraft in combat. By contrast, the Germans were able to call upon a large pool of well-trained aircrew – a decisive factor once casualties began to mount.

The German Official History of the Invasion referred to the opening phase of the epic fight for aerial mastery as the *Kannalkampf* or Channel Battle. As the first units of Luftflotte 2 arrived at their airfields in northern France, they were instructed to attack the British convoys sailing up and down the English Channel. These tactics were partly intended to put a stop to British maritime traffic in the Channel, but more importantly, they were employed as a way of drawing Fighter Command into battle over the Channel. In addition, it would give the air crews a taste of combat against a largely unknown enemy, and as German numbers increased, units were rotated accordingly. Finally, in order to test RAF defences sporadic attacks were mounted against inland targets.

The British response was to husband resources consistent with defending the Channel convoys and intercepting German raids. For both sides the first two weeks of June were a period of experiment and assessment. The Germans were disconcerted by the British ability to intercept, and General Martini and the other Luftwaffe technical experts soon realized that the tall aerial masts dotted along the English coast – some visible from France – were perhaps part of a sophisticated interception system. Their positions were logged in preparation for destruction once the next phase of the battle was joined.

The intensity of the fighting increased as more Luftwaffe units were committed to the attack on British convoys. Protected by an umbrella of fighters, the German bomber *Geschwaders* began to disrupt this Channel traffic, causing significant losses on the British destroyer escorts operating from Dover. Also, the mid-Channel scraps which developed between RAF and Luftwaffe favoured the Germans. They could always choose when to attack (a strategic initiative maintained throughout the battle) and their fighters were operating closer to home than those of Fighter Command.

Fearful of dissipating his fighter strength, Dowding pressed for the abandonment of Channel convoys – always more a matter of prestige than economic necessity – but his pleas were ignored until 26 June when shipping losses finally forced the Admiralty into calling a halt. Following his decision was the order to transfer the destroyers of the Dover Flotilla from their exposed position in the Channel Narrows to the relative safety of Sheerness and Portsmouth. In the light of the losses suffered by the Dover Flotilla (five destroyers sunk, three severely damaged) it was a reasonable decision but one which facilitated the passage of the German invasion fleet through the Straits of Dover.

By the end of June over 2,500 Luftwaffe aircraft were assembled for action. Although Göring was swift to take maximum credit for any Luftwaffe victory, German aerial success was largely due to the work of Kesselring and his gifted and experienced subordinate commanders of Luftflotte 2.

The second phase of the German plan, *Adlerangriff* or Eagle Attack, would be an offensive of rising intensity. The destruction of Fighter Command remained central to the Luftwaffe plan, to be achieved through aerial combat and the destruction of airfields and other RAF installations (including the Radar stations). Secondary attacks were to be directed against coastal towns, but the Luftwaffe bomber commanders were instructed to be mindful in the selection of targets, for it was expected that the Wehrmacht would be using Britain's ports for their own purposes in the near future.

The 1 July had been selected as *Adlertag* (Eagle Day) but the second phase did not effectively begin until two days later when more than 600 aircraft were launched against RAF airfields in south-east England. As it assembled over France, the size of the force was visible on British Radar screens. A large

Right One of the most vital elements of the British defensive system, an Observer Corps centre table plotting known sightings of German aircraft.

Below right RAF fighter pilots of 610 Squadron relax beside their Spitfires but ready at any moment for the call to 'Scramble!'

Below A classic propaganda shot of a German Messerschmitt Bf 109 set against the chalk cliffs of southern England. That German fighters were able to fly along the Channel coast with virtual impunity by the end of June relected their success in the *Kannalkampf.*

number of 11 Group squadrons were scrambled, so that when the Germans crossed the coast above Folkestone they were met by an angry swarm of Spitfires and Hurricanes. German casualties mounted: the Spitfires took on the German fighters while the Hurricanes broke into the bomber formations, where their eight .303-inch machine guns wreaked havoc. Some of the more badly shot-up bomber *Geschwaders* were forced to jettison their bombs; others pressed on to their targets. The coastal airfields of Manston, Hawkinge and Lympne were all hit hard. Further inland Biggin Hill and Gravesend received only light damage. The Luftwaffe lost 18 bombers and 11 fighters in its first major raid. The RAF figure of 15 aircraft shot down reflected the skill of the German fighter escorts, although of these, six pilots parachuted to safety – one of the advantages of fighting over home territory.

Poor weather prevented further German attacks that day, allowing the Luftwaffe commanders to re-examine their tactics in the light of relatively heavy losses. Previous forays over mainland England had usually been swiftly and effectively intercepted; the 3 July attack underlined the efficiency of the British defensive system. The staff officers of Luftflotte 2 realized that they must swamp British defences by launching successive waves of aircraft to confuse the RAF sector controllers who directed the Fighter Command squadrons. If nothing else, the sheer weight of numbers would wear down the RAF, who in a battle of attrition must inevitably lose. Such tactics would place an incredible strain on the Luftwaffe but if their objectives were to be achieved in time for S-Day on 13 July, there could be no hesitation.

The next big attack was launched on 5 July.

Above far left The unmistakable sight of the masts of a Radar 'Chain Home' station, a vital target for German bombers.
Far left Hurricanes of 501 Squadron take off to intercept a German attack, 16 July 1940.
Above left German air staff standing on the cliffs of the Pas de Calais welcome the return of a Junkers Ju 87 Stuka after a ground attack mission against British radar stations.
Left: A *Geschwader* of Heinkel He 111s takes up formation prior to leading a bombing run against RAF Fighter Command airfields.

Above left Adolf Galland, along with Werner Mölders the top German ace in the fight against the RAF.

Left Luftwaffe air control staff signal a successful strike against a target in Britain.

Above An example of a German raid on an RAF airfield. Although there were many more easier targets, it was this relentless attack against Fighter Command that finally brought the Luftwaffe victory.

Involving all three Luftflotten, the Germans flew over 2,000 sorties in one day. This time they attacked the Radar stations. If the tall RD masts proved surprisingly resistant to the effects of blast, the wooden structures housing the stations were appropriately vulnerable. By midday the stations at Rye, Pevensey, Poling and Ventnor had gone off the air, leaving a vast gap over southern England, through which poured the Luftwaffe air fleets. Germans listening in on British radio transmissions were gratified to hear the confusion between controllers and fighter squadrons unable to find their targets. Although the stations were back on air the next day, repeated Luftwaffe attacks critically reduced the effectiveness of the whole system from 5 July onwards.

In the air, the outnumbered Fighter Command squadrons fought with great determination, inflicting heavy casualties when they caught the bomber formations. However, they were unable to prevent the Luftwaffe from getting through to its targets on most occasions. During raids on 7 July German bombers badly hit RAF squadrons on the ground, and by the end of the day the casualty ratio was to their advantage: 55 British aircraft (including 42 fighters) against a loss of 34 bombers and 13 fighters.

Each day, weather permitting, the Luftwaffe threw itself against the RAF with the utmost ferocity. The senior Luftwaffe commanders had noted a slackening of Fighter Command's response to their attacks, but were forced to admit to Göring that they could not guarantee complete aerial mastery over England by 13 July. Göring raved at his officers, demanding that they redouble their efforts to subdue the RAF, but he accepted the facts of the situation, even though he realized they would not be well received at the major OKW conference on 9 July.

As the German service chiefs met with Hitler in Berlin, Göring's pride was saved by Admiral Raeder's prompt admission that despite 'superhuman efforts' by the Kriegsmarine, the invasion fleet would no be ready to sail on 13 July. Raeder was adamant that there should be a postponement, and despite Army protests (but with support from Göring) the date was extended to 23 July – when tides and suitable moonlight would allow amphibious operations. This 10-day extension enabled the Luftwaffe to complete its mission.

Unseasonally bad weather hampered the Luftwaffe's efforts in the two weeks leading up to the invasion date, but Göring refused to spare his men and attacks were made every day, major offensives every two or three days. For the RAF the strain was becoming unbearable. Raw recruits were being pushed into combat, only to become cannon fodder for the guns of the German fighters, leaving behind a decreasing group of exhausted veterans to carry on the fight. Morale began to suffer; not so much among the pilots who fought on to the end, but among ground crew who cracked under these relentless attacks. At Manston ground staff refused to leave their slit trenches, leaving the pilots to rearm and service their aircraft.

By the middle of July the tide of battle had turned in the Germans' favour and packs of their bombers were allowed to roam over south-east England without interference. For the Luftwaffe crews the 'happy time' had begun. One German ace summarized this change of fortune:

'Our first experience of the English Spitfires came as a great shock to us all, and our comrades in the bombers were not slow in reproaching us for the heavy casualties they were suffering. But eventually we gained the measure of our opponents; their Radar could not save them in the end. Regardless of almost total physical and mental exhaustion, our fighter and bomber crews pressed the enemy relentlessly, and our superior numbers and training did the rest.'

Dowding had fought the battle to the best of his abilities, but on 12 July he had been forced to abandon the coastal airfields of Manston, Hawkinge, Lympne and Tangmere. A week later fighter squadrons were withdrawn to bases north of London. This fateful order was tacit acknowledgement by Fighter Command that they were losing the battle. Long-range fighter cover along Britain's Channel coast could only be mounted sporadically, giving the Germans virtual air superiority over the invasion sector.

Pressure on the RAF was maintained in the last couple of days before the invasion fleet left port, while the Luftwaffe simultaneously began its next phase – attacks on communication centres in southeast England and the softening up of coastal defences around the invasion beaches. Other raids, ranging from Dorset to Suffolk, disguised German intentions. The Luftwaffe would be on hand to support the Navy and Army when the time came.

INVASION

During the final few days before S-Day on 23 July both sides experienced deep concern. The staff officers of General Busch's Sixteenth Army wrestled with the multiplicity of problems thrown up by an amphibious attack. The British realized an invasion was imminent but they were still not sure where or when.

To the German High Command on S-1 the prognosis seemed healthy: the Luftwaffe had beaten, if not destroyed, the RAF; the Kriegsmarine had assembled sufficient craft; the Army confirmed its readiness for action; and weather prospects looked good. The order was given – Operation Sea Lion was finally underway.

Late in the afternoon of 22 July coastal vessels were spotted by RAF reconnaissance aircraft moving westward from Rotterdam along the Belgian coast. The British were not unduly concerned, preferring to see it as the resumption of normal commercial business. The apparently innocent craft were in fact the first wave of the German fleet sailing from Holland and Belgium. As night fell other vessels slipped secretly from their harbours to join the main stream heading towards the English coast.

The Germans had maintained the strictest secur-ity throughout the period leading up to S-Day. Deception measures had helped distract British attention from the invasion fleet. The German Sixth Army had been maintained in north-west Europe in order to disguise the destination of the attack. On S-1 the harbours of Brittany and Normandy were alive with activity as a number of old steamships were overtly made ready for sea, leaving port in the general direction of south-west England and Ireland. From Norway the heavy cruiser *Hipper* had set sail for the gap between Scotland and Iceland while other German naval craft seemed to be heading towards northern England.

The decoy forces were intercepted by the British on the night of the invasion and quickly turned tail to steam back to their home ports. The effectiveness of these measures is hard to assess, but the main force was not spotted by the British until only two hours before S-Hour at 4 am – too late to mount immediate and effective seaborne opposition.

When the first British patrol boats saw the enemy vessels in the moonlight, they shot off their emergency signal flares and plunged into the enemy mass to do what damage they could before their own inevitable destruction. Within minutes other British

Right Spearhead of the invasion, a German paratrooper hurls a grenade towards a British position, 23 July 1940. The speed with which the 7th (Air) Division secured the high ground above Folkestone and Hythe was an important factor in ensuring the success of the seaborne landings; the startled British defenders on the shore found themselves under attack from front and rear.

The moment of truth: German soldiers of the 35th Infantry Division hit the beaches on the morning of S-Day. Although training for the landings had been rudimentary, the assault troops were only too aware of the need to race inland, away from the danger zone on the shoreline.

Above German staff officers watch elements of the invasion fleet moving down the English Channel on S-Day; the white cliffs of Dover are visible in the background. While other senior officers remained at their various headquarters, Göring (sixth from right) could not resist motoring over to the Pas de Calais to observe proceedings.

Right Light escort vessels of the invasion fleet maintain a careful eye for intervention from the Royal Navy. Although the British response was swift in coming, the combined forces of the Luftwaffe and Kriegsmarine were sufficient to prevent serious disruption of the landings.

light craft were on the scene but were either held off or sunk by the German escorts. As first light glimmered at 3.30 am, the soldiers afloat caught the sound of the steady drone of transport aircraft – the airborne attack going in.

The 7th Air (*Flieger*) Division fielded only 10,000 men – as against 18,000 of the regular divisions – and lacked heavy weapons, but still remained a formidable combat organization. The paratroopers were among the toughest soldiers in the German armed forces and, at strategic level, the division's aerial mobility was a trump card in the hands of a skilful general.

Preceding the main paratroop force was a smaller unit of gliderborne troops. Their function was to secure Hawkinge airfield, using the silence of the glider descent to ensure complete surprise. The eight DFS 230 gliders landed in and around the British airfield at 3 am on 23 July – the first German troops on British soil. The small and startled British garrison had been taken entirely by surprise and were easily overwhelmed by the paratroops. Minutes later the first wave of Junkers Ju 52 transports began to disgorge their cargoes of paratroops, the lead elements of three regiments who would secure the high ground above Folkestone and Hythe while their seaborne comrades landed on the beaches below.

Looking upwards in the dawn light, the British defenders witnessed the extraordinary sight of an airborne invasion in progress, the sky a mass of opening parachutes. The wind was fairly light and the navigation sound, so the 7th Air Division's landing was not badly dispersed. Some of the descending paratroops, however, were caught and slaughtered by British units in the immediate vicinity. But these were isolated instances and once on the ground the paratroops swiftly formed up and silenced any opposition. By 6.30 am the paratroops had secured the high ground from Densole through Hawkinge and Paddlesworth to Etchinghill. During the next four hours the westerly line from Newington, Sandling Station and Westenhanger to Lympne (with its small satellite airfield) would fall to the airborne forces. Meanwhile the battle for the beaches raged.

As the paratroops were fighting for the heights, the German invasion fleet was approaching the shore. The most critical part of the German attack was against Hythe on 'B' Beach, the position of honour taken by the experienced 17th Infantry Division under the command of Major-General Herbert Loch.

As the fleet made its 'right turn' towards the shore, the big guns from Dover began to find their targets. Fortunately for the invaders, the guns were few in number and their accuracy was reduced by smoke screens laid by the German escorts. The arrival of the 300 German bombers over 'B' Beach (including nearly 150 Ju 87 Stuka dive bombers) was perfectly on cue. They plastered the defences from Dover to New Romney, keeping British heads down during the critical first hour of the assault. In addition, the enormous German long-range guns were firing their salvoes of high explosive into Folkestone and Hythe from positions on the French coast.

The first German troops had clambered into their stormboats a little after 4 am to race the last few hundred yards to the shore. Once on dry land, the Germans struggled up the shingle beach to the sea wall where were pinned down by a barrage of smallarms and machine-gun fire. Meanwhile, German assault engineers were furiously clearing the beach of defensive obstacles, suffering heavy casualties in the process.

To the British the invasion fleet may have looked formidable, but for the German flotilla commanders the task of getting their unwieldy prahms to the shore was a serious struggle. Units were completely mixed up and the Siebel craft which were supposed to provide fire support had, for the most part, fallen back out of sight. As the prahms began to move towards land, the shuttle service of stormboats from minesweepers to shore continued, although both types of vessel were being hit by British fire.

The survivors of the battle for the beaches recalled in detail the scenes of the morning of 23 July. On land, sea and air the fight raged with growing intensity. Amongst the Germans huddled alongside the seawall at Sandgate (between Hythe and Folkstone) was a young company commander, who spoke of his experiences:

'My men and I had managed to reach the shore with few losses but once on the beach we had to cut our way through coils of barbed wire, supposedly cut by the Luftwaffe's Stukas. It was then that we suffered many casualties to an English machine-gun positioned in a cylindrical tower. This I later learned was a Martello Tower, built to repel Napoleon's threatened invasion; though the irony of this would not have been appreciated by us at the time! Around us was sheer pandemonium. Looking up, I could see our transport aircraft returning home, some going down in flames, while

Above The DFS 230 was capable of gliding up to 40 miles from a release point at 12,000 feet, and held a crew of 10 men. As had happened at Eban Emael in May, the silent approach of the gliders caught the defenders completely by surprise.

Left A rare photograph taken by a British soldier guarding Hawkinge airfield on the morning of 23 July; German paratroopers leap from Junkers Ju 52 transport aircraft.

directly above our dive bombers were circling for another attack. Out at sea the splashes of enemy shells were making their pattern amongst the incoming craft. I feel we would have remained on the shingle and pebbles of that wretched beach for ever had not small groups – led by engineers with flame throwers and explosive charges – forced their way over the wall and fought their way into the town.'

To the assault troops of the 17th Infantry Division the British defences along the seafront around

Hythe seemed strong. In fact they consisted only of a reinforced company of the Royal West Kent Regiment. Although they put up a bitter fight, causing the attackers severe casualties, they were desperately outnumbered, and once sufficient Germans had crossed over the sea wall their resistance crumbled. Once past this obstacle, the German vanguard began to fight its way through Hythe and eastward into Folkestone, while the main body of the Division landed from the now beached prahms.

To the west of Hythe the remainder of the 17th Division raced across the beach, facing little opposition until reaching the Royal Military Canal where a fierce fire-fight developed. Here the Germans received unexpected assistance from the Luftwaffe's élite Operational Proving Unit 210, whose Bf 110s and 109s had been especially converted for the role of ground-fighting. The Messerschmitts roared at tree-top level, dispersing the British resistance and allowing the German infantry to gain the high ground around West Hythe, linking up with the paratroops advancing from the north-east at Lympne airfield.

The divisional boundary of the XIII Corps was the Great Redoubt (another old Napoleonic fortification) which was swiftly taken. The long beach line sloping away from the Redoubt was the responsibility of the 35th Infantry Division. British defences were easily overcome, even if the interlocking Martello Tower system caused initial trouble. Here the Germans were aided by amphibious tanks. Although many PzKpfw IIIs tanks foundered on the beaches and the high sea wall, a dozen broke through the defences at Dymchurch, their 3.7cm main guns providing valuable fire support. Operating alongside the infantry, the German tanks moved northward along the roads criss-crossing the old Romney Marshes to gain control of the scarp slope the far side of the Royal Military Canal. In places the British line was over 300 feet above the land below and, to the Germans on the Marshes, seemed almost cliff-like. But the sudden arrival of the German armour came as a shock to the British on the heights. Surprised and outnumbered, they fell back towards Ashford after only a token fight.

The 35th Division had not been severely tested in the initial battle although its staff officers had enormous problems imposing order on the confusion of units arriving (or not arriving) on the beaches. For example, the bicycle battalion which was supposed to land early in the First Wave consisted of little

more than a company's worth of troops, who were despatched across the Marshes to link up with advance elements of the 7th Infantry Division, due to land to the west of Dungeness.

Despite the difficulties experienced by the 35th Infantry Division, the XIII Corps was broadly keeping to the timetable, but the VII Corps was experiencing almost all the problems of an amphibious operation gone wrong. Mechanical failures and navigational errors had been more serious than those of the other corps. The lead elements of the 1st Mountain Division landed some 50 minutes late, but the 7th Infantry Division experienced a nightmare landing: some units arrived alongside the mountain troops, others drifted around to the east of Dungeness, while less than half the division was landed as planned on the beaches of Rye Bay.

The men of the 7th Infantry Division managed to secure the immediate shore-line running from Camber Sands to Winchelsea Beach but quickly became bogged down as they tried to advance towards the high ground dominated by the old towns of Winchelsea and Rye. Although repeatedly battered by waves of Luftwaffe bombs, the British defenders were well dug in and easily repulsed the somewhat confused German assaults. By midday Winchelsea had been taken – at considerable loss to the attackers

Above Protected by well-laid smoke screens, German assault troops race to the beach in their high-powered stormboats, capable of covering the final dash at 25 knots. Despite their speed the stormboats were highly vulnerable to British smallarms fire, and many were lost during the initial stages of the assault.

– but Rye and the ridge of high land running east of the town remained in British hands. For Lieutenant General Freiherr von Gablenz, commander of the 7th Infantry Division, it was a difficult moment; unless Rye was in German hands an effective beach-head could not be established and a dangerous gap between the 35th Infantry and 1st Mountain Divisions would develop.

During the day staff officers of the 7th Infantry Division began to impose some sort of order on their troops, and finally the divisional allotment of artillery and tanks was assembled. At 2 pm German 7.5cm howitzers began to fire on Rye, and following another pounding from the Luftwaffe, a combined infantry-armour attack was launched against the stubborn British defenders. The ridge positions of Udimore and Cock Marling were the first to fall, and as the Germans pushed forward Rye became increasingly isolated.

The commander of two companies of a Rifle Brigade battalion holding the now smoking ruins of Rye repeatedly refused to surrender. By late afternoon, the Germans were fighting their way through the streets of the town while the few remaining inhabitants cowered in their houses. Shortly after the fall of the old Ypres Tower at 4.30 pm, British resistance came to an end. Rye had been sacked before, by French raiders in 1420 during the Hundred Years' War, but the 1940 attackers were intent on outright occupation rather than mere pillage.

The German assault troops were exhausted by the unexpected struggle. Meanwhile a detachment of PzKpfw II light tanks raced directly northward in an

Top right German combat engineers cut a passage through barbed-wire defences surrounding Rye. The British garrison holding the old Cinque port put up stubborn resistance.

Above right German infantry scramble across the rocks alongside Fairlight Cove.

Right Having secured the crossing at Botolph's Bridge on the Romney Marshes, this assault group races forward to gain the high ground near Lympne.

attempt to secure their first objective of Tenterden. But as darkness fell, the tank commander called a halt at Wittersham on the Isle of Oxney.

Further west along the coast, the 1st Mountain Division experienced a morning of mixed fortunes. Co-operating with troops from the 7th Infantry Division, the right flank of the Mountain Division took heavy casualties as it fought its way off the beach at Cliff End. When resistance at Winchelsea was overcome, the mountain troops were able to advance inland to Icklesham without delay. The cliffs below Fairlight were considered gravely hazardous by the Germans. British defences were virtually non-existent, however, and the Alpine-trained Germans had little trouble scaling the wooded slopes around Fairlight Glen. Once on high ground, the mountain troops consolidated their position before turning west to aid their comrades on the extreme left flank engaged in a bloody battle for the seafront at Hastings.

The British troops defending Hastings were prepared for the German stormboats as they made their final run for shore. Concentrated machine-gun fire dealt with boat after boat. Of the few that made it to the beach, their occupants were shot down in the surf. Thus, the ungainly prahms made their way ashore against a fully defended coastline. British artillery pieces in and around Hastings were making their presence felt. To the horror of German on-lookers, the slow-moving prahms were suffering repeated hits and a number could be seen sinking with the loss of hundreds of men and vital equipment. On witnessing a few successful landings away from the seafront, near to the old town, the German naval commander redeployed his forces. Unable to call back all the prahms, he redirected enough vessels to enlarge the tenuous beach-head below the old town.

By now the mountain troops who had landed at Fairlight Glen were advancing through the outskirts of Hastings, and light but accurate mortar fire was landing on the British along the seafront. From their old town base German forces were infiltrating British positions. Eventually the defenders – by now grossly outnumbered – were forced to conduct a fighting retreat through the town. By the end of S-Day the tired but relieved general of the 1st Mountain Division was able to report to his corps commander that his men had secured Hastings and had advanced several kilometres inland to establish the basis for an effective beach-head.

Even though the 1st Mountain and 7th Infantry Divisions had suffered heavy casualties and failed to

Top A German destroyer lays a smoke screen to cover the landing operations between Folkestone and Hythe.

Above centre German mountain troops set up a 7.5cm mountain gun in support of the attack on Fairlight Glen.

Above German infantry race across the levels between Icklesham and Cock Marling. Once the ridge Udimore-Cock Marling was in German hands, Rye could be attacked from the flank.

fully achieve their first-day objectives, they were ashore and in position. The main fight of the day had always been intended for the two divisions on the extreme right flank – 7th Air and 17th Infantry – and it was on these formations that success or defeat would ultimately depend.

Once off the beaches, the troops of the 17th Infantry Division advanced through Hythe, eliminating isolated pockets of British resistance as they fought their way to meet up with the paratroops of the 7th Air Division holding a fragile line to the north of Folkestone and Hythe. General Loch had insisted on arriving in the forefront of his 17th Division, so he was able to discuss the next stage of operation with the paratroop commander, Major-General Puitzier. They met at around 3 pm and, agreeably surprised at their success, they decided to press on without delay to their first major objective, the capture of Dover. Plans for a direct attack on this vital harbour town, with its excellent seaward defences, had been rejected in favour of a flank attack.

Holding units were left at Lyminge and Densole, while advance elements of the paratroops' 19th Regiment and the 17th Division's 55th Regiment

Above The seafront along Hastings beach on S+1, a desolate scene of death and destruction.

Above left A gun from a British coastal battery shells the invasion fleet on the afternoon of 23 July.

Left A German 3.7cm anti-tank gun is manoeuvred over the rubble of recently destroyed buildings, as the 17th Infantry Division presses on to the heart of Dover.

advanced directly on Dover, with a few remaining tanks in tow. At sea the big Dover guns had been kept occupied by the returning vessels of the invasion fleet and the seemingly foolhardy emergence of two old German First World War battleships, *Schlesien* and *Schleswig-Holstein*. The two obsolete warships pounded away at British positions around Dover, drawing the landward-based fire with deadly effect. By early evening both ships were reduced to burning hulks. As sacrificial lambs they had served their purpose well, drawing fire away from the returning invasion fleet, but the loss of the two ships and the deaths of over 1,100 seaman was deeply felt by the Kriegsmarine.

Grabbing what local transport it could, lead elements of the 19th Parachute Regiment raced along the valley road past Alkham towards the railway halt at Kearsney, north of Dover. The remainder of the regiment followed on as best it could. On the main coast road between Folkestone and Dover, the 55th Regiment was advancing with equal rapidity. The paratroops cut Dover off from the north, the main attack falling on the port as evening fell. Meanwhile the Luftwaffe had delivered an enormous hour-long attack on the town, beginning at 6.30 pm.

As the German troops closed with the defenders, the sky was lit by the flames which engulfed the port. Along with the fires caused by the German bombing, the British naval authorities were making a systematic attempt to destroy all port facilities. The men of the 17th Infantry Division slowly forced the British garrison back through the town. After the fall of Priory Station at 2.30 am on 24 July, British resistance crumbled. As S+1 dawned, the town was in German hands. Much of the harbour area was in ruins, but German naval and engineer experts were confident that the port could be sufficiently cleared to allow the unloading of heavy stores within a couple of days.

On hearing the news of the fall of Dover, a delighted Hitler radioed over the award of the Knight's Cross to General Loch – the first of many during the campaign.

At the local level the British response to the German invasion had failed, but this was inevitable given the disparity of forces. By the end of the first day the German Sixteenth Army had established a beach-head. Now the British would have to assemble sufficient forces to throw the Germans back into the sea, while the Royal Navy concentrated all its power on cutting the invaders off from their lifeline to the Continent.

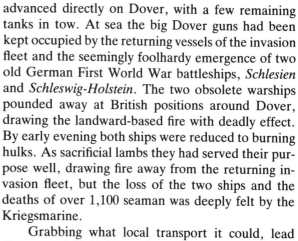

Above A squadron of RAF Spitfires deployed in formation line abreast, cruising at 300 mph between cloud layers at 6,000 feet. The casualties suffered by the RAF in late July were so great, however, they could do little to hamper the progress of the invasion forces.

During 23 July both fighters and bombers of the RAF had thrown themselves at the invaders, but the Luftwaffe maintained an iron ring around the air space over south-east England. Flying from airfields deep in the heart of England, the Spitfires and Hurricanes were stretched to the limits of their fuel endurance and could only provide minimal support for the bombers. While the Bf 109s dealt with the British fighters, the powerfully armed Bf 110s slaughtered the almost defenceless Whitleys, Blenheims and Hampdens.

Aware of the desperate gravity of the situation, the British pilots flew on regardless of casualties. In a single day the RAF lost 47 bombers, 32 precious single-seat fighters and 12 other aircraft. The sad truth was that only two squadrons managed to make anything like successful bombing runs – against targets in Folkestone and Hastings – and the degree of disruption to the Germans on both occasions was negligible. The fighter leader (*Jafü*) of Luftflotte 2 viewed the British performance from his own Bf 109 and aptly dubbed it the 'death charge of the RAF'.

The Royal Navy's reponse was more rapid. By 8 am on the day of the invasion, destroyer flotillas were racing out from their bases at Portsmouth and Nore. As they approached the enemy, however, their progress was severely hampered by a succession of expertly sown minefields. After the loss of two destroyers from each flotilla, the slow-moving British vessels fell victim to Luftwaffe dive-bombing attacks. In the face of such a strong aerial attack, the Nore flotilla, its flagship crippled, was forced back to base. The Portsmouth flotilla managed to get within striking distance of the invasion fleet. By now, however, the British counter-attack had been reduced to four undamaged destroyers and, in the face of determined German naval resistance, the British were beaten back, having caused only minor damage. Out of an original force of 11 destroyers, just six battered vessels limped back to Portsmouth on the 24th. After the repulse of the British light forces, the Navy was compelled to place its faith in the heavy units steaming southward from their base in Scapa Flow.

The Kriegsmarine had always feared the arrival of the Royal Navy's capital ships, and when reconnaissance aircraft sighted *Nelson*, *Valiant* and *Repulse* with attendant escorts south of the Humber on the morning of 25 July, Raeder and his staff almost panicked. Following a personal call from Raeder, Göring promised his full support and exhausted Luftwaffe crews were redeployed away from the land battle to attack the British capital ships.

Supported by cruisers and destroyers from Nore Command, the British waited until nightfall before entering the narrows around Dover, thus negating Luftwaffe superiority. A last-minute burst of speed by the British ships caught the Germans by surprise, although one British cruiser and two destroyers were lost to German mines. Once inside the German defensive screen, the British cruisers and destroyers began to sink the German supply ships in mid-Channel, and as the *Hipper* and *Köln* attempted to come to their aid both were blown out of the water by a furious bombardment from the British capital ships.

While the various elements of the German fleet scurried to the nearest available ports, the British shelled German shipping in Calais and Boulogne before withdrawing at dawn, only too aware of Luft-

Above The devastating power of a salvo of 15-inch shells from HMS *Warspite* can be seen in this photograph of the Battle of the Narrows. In less than five minutes *Warspite*, supported by *Nelson* and *Repulse*, had sunk both *Hipper* and *Köln*.

Right General Herbert Loch, commander of the 17th Infantry Division, pictured after the award of the Knight's Cross (worn at neck) for the capture of Dover.

waffe superiority in daylight. For the next few days, the Germans suspended night convoys but the Royal Navy was unable to operate in daylight. Given the long daylight hours of July, the Germans again held the advantage and although disrupted, vital supplies continued to arrive by sea.

In the last pre-invasion staff meeting the German divisional commanders had been instructed by Busch to dig in once a reasonable position had been gained. As the Germans had expected, the British infantry fought stoutly but lacked tactical sophistication. Busch's generals were reasonably confident that they could weather the storm of British counter-attacks.

The fact that substantial German forces had been able to establish themselves on British soil after a single day's battle came as a grave shock to General

Below Armed with a combination of .303 rifles and Bren light machine guns, a company of British infantry prepares to defend its hedgerow position against a German attack, 24 July 1940. Although the British troops fought with the utmost resolution, they lacked adequate support and their counter-attacks were badly co-ordinated. As a result casualties were heavy and progress limited.

Right One of the deadly 8.8cm dual-purpose guns in action. Originally designed for anti-aircraft use, the Germans quickly discovered how effective they were when used in an anti-tank role. Although somewhat bulky, the high-velocity gun could fire a 9.5kg (21 lb) shell capable of penetrating any British armoured vehicle — including the Matilda — at even the longest ranges.

Sir Alan Brooke. The Prime Minister urged his armed forces to deal with the aggressor without delay. Brooke would have preferred a more carefully planned offensive but, under pressure from Churchill, ordered Major-General Evans to launch an immediate attack with his 1st Armoured Division. Understrength after its battering in France, and based deep in Surrey, the British tank forces only began to move forward towards the end of S-day.

The bulk of the division moved by train but was forced to disembark at Tonbridge and Maidstone as a consequence of the Luftwaffe's destruction of rail communications. The tanks' progress by road was continuously blocked by processions of refugees. Only towards the end of 24 July (S+1) did the first tanks reach German lines around Tenterden. Two British cruiser tanks were immediately destroyed by well-positioned German anti-tank guns, although in the exchange of fire three German tanks were hit by Matildas for no further British loss. Nightfall brought an end to the engagement, the main battle postponed to the following day.

Warned of the arrival of the British 1st Armoured Division, the Germans took appropriate steps to neutralize the threat. The Luftwaffe was briefed of British tank dispositions, and the 8.8cm dual-purpose guns were rushed to the front line. On the second day of the invasion the German ground forces had only reached positions deemed essential to absorb a counter-attack.

General Evans's plan consisted of a two-pronged thrust, each led by the heavily armoured Matildas, supported by whatever infantry was available. From the moment the British tanks advanced from their night laagers, they were attacked by the Luftwaffe, a disruption that delayed the assault until late morning.

The Matildas broke through the enemy front lines with comparative ease, the shot from the German 3.7cm anti-tank guns bouncing off their well-armoured hulls. After penetrating the German positions for a few miles, the British advance began to slow as infantry support faded away. At this point the high-velocity 8.8cm guns came into play. Suddenly the Matildas were vulnerable and the German guns caused havoc, forcing the surviving British tanks to withdraw.

The other British tank types – Cruiser and Light Tank – were easily stopped. British artillery, in short supply and without sufficient ammunition, could do little to support the numerous infantry attacks launched along the German line. Against first-class troops the badly-co-ordinated British counter-attack failed completely.

For the British 25 July was a black day. The German beach-head was intact, all attacks repulsed with ease. The British Command could do little but reorganize its forces, although the most probable development in the campaign would be the German breakout. If the British were unable to hold this next move the war would be almost certainly lost.

GERMAN BREAKOUT AND VICTORY

Hitler was later to tell sycophantic audiences that 23 July had been the most stressful day of his life. When reports of the early setback of VII Corps on the German left flank had reached OKW, it seemed to Hitler and the more pessimistic of his staff that the invasion would fail. Never had Hitler gambled so much and it was only after news of the capture of Dover and the establishment of a firm defensive line reached him that he could look to the future with confidence. On 25 July, as the last echelons of the First Wave crossed the Channel, Hitler sanctioned deployment of the Second Wave.

The failure of the British counter-attack on the 25th came as a major blow to Churchill. While rallying the country with nightly broadcasts, he privately suffered the greatest anguish. At a tense meeting with the Chiefs-of-Staff, Churchill impressed upon them his desire to overcome this initial setback and carry on the fight with renewed determination. They agreed to speed up the reinforcement of British troops in the invasion area ready for a second assault – although only when the Army commanders on the ground considered it capable of success.

On 27 July, the remnants of the 1st London and 45th Divisions holding the line against the now quiescent German positions, were joined by the 52nd and 1st Canadian Divisions. The 1st Armoured Division was reinforced by the arrival of the 2nd Armoured Division on the 28th, although this formation was both inexperienced and poorly equipped. The 43rd and 2nd London Divisions moved out of East Anglia to act as a central reserve south-west of London.

Three divisions remained in East Anglia, however, partly because of the activities of the Brandenburg Battalion. These German Special Forces troops (under the control of German Army Intelligence) had made several raids on the coast between Lowestoft and Southend (25–28 July) and Eastern Command was especially wary of leaving this strategically vital area poorly defended.

Within the beach-head the Germans set about consolidating their gains, reorganizing their defences and preparing for the arrival of reinforcements. The swift capture of Hawkinge and Lympne airfields ensured the shuttle sevice of Ju 52s, protected by Bf 109s, was operable by S+1. The Luftwaffe fleet of nearly 500 transports (although diminishing every day due to accidents and enemy action) flew twice

Right German armoured units advance over the downlands of southern England, August 1940. Unlike the British, the Germans skilfully integrated tanks and infantry in both attack and defence. The lead tank is a Czech-built PzKpfw 35(t), many of which had been pressed into German service after the invasion of Czechoslovakia.

72·BRITAIN INVADED

Above The crew of a forward machine-gun post take cover from a British artillery bombardment.

Left French dockers work on the quayside, loading one of the many transport ships taking supplies across the Channel as part of the German build-up prior to breakout.

daily when weather conditions allowed. This ensured a steady supply of munitions and the arrival of the 22nd Air Landing Division (conventional troops trained in aerial transportation) between 24 and 27 July.

Despite the efficiency of the German aerial supply system – unknown to the British at the time – it was only through traditional maritime reinforcement that the Sixteenth Army was able to build up the armoured force essential for victory. Amongst the First Wave were the engineers – Army and Navy – who were detailed to restore the damaged ports without delay. Folkestone Harbour was secured almost intact. In full operation from S+1 onward it remained a useful if limited supply route, capable of handling a few hundred tons a day. The small outlet

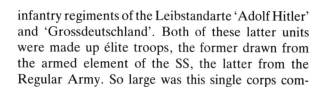

Above Under the supervision of German troops, wounded Canadian soldiers are led away into captivity, 29 July 1940. Alongside the Canadians there were contingents of Australians and New Zealanders fighting in Britain during the summer of 1940 — as well as units of exiled French, Poles and Czechs.

of Rye Harbour, however, was limited by its dependence on the tide. Dover was the key to the German logistical system, and once a couple of safe channels had been cleared through the sabotaged port on 27 July, the transhipment of the Second Wave became a sound proposition.

The arrival of the Royal Navy's heavy units off Dover on the night of 24–25 July had slowed the rate of incoming German supplies, but after it had been proved to the nervous German maritime forces that the Luftwaffe's aerial domination prevented the Royal Navy from operating off the Narrows except in the hours of darkness, a steady daylight stream of cross-Channel shipping developed.

After the extraordinary successes gained by the German panzer divisions during the French campaign, even the most conservative German generals were convinced of their ability to snatch victory from conventional opponents. Rundstedt and Busch had decided that the Second Wave should consist of a massive armoured force.

General Reinhardt was reunited with his XXXXI Panzer Corps, now comprising 3rd Panzer, 10th Panzer and 29th Motorized Divisions, to which was added 7th Panzer Division (from XVth Corps of the Ninth Army) and the reinforced motorized

infantry regiments of the Leibstandarte 'Adolf Hitler' and 'Grossdeutschland'. Both of these latter units were made up élite troops, the former drawn from the armed element of the SS, the latter from the Regular Army. So large was this single corps command that it was soon renamed Panzer Group Reinhardt.

Between 26 July and 2 August, the men and vehicles of the Second Wave were brought ashore. Despite pressure from both OKH and OKW, Busch insisted on a proper build-up of forces, and only when the bulk of Panzer Group Reinhardt was on the English side of the Channel did he agree upon 3 August as the date for the breakout. By then over 600 tanks would be in position.

Alongside preparations for the coming panzer

assault, the Germans were also busy administering the coastal strip that was now German-occupied Britain. The German attitude towards the civilian population was severe in the extreme. During the fighting the German armed forces left the local inhabitants more or less alone (apart from commandeering useful war materials) but any signs of resistance met with stern reprisal. Although the majority of civilians had either been evacuated or fled, some remained. The horrors of the recent fighting cowed most of them into a state of sullen resignation, but some inevitably found the yoke of military occupation too much to bear.

The German military authorities did not recognize the Home Guard/Local Defence Volunteer and when youths wearing LDV armbands were caught sniping at a passing German column they were shot out of hand. Hostages were then taken locally as a guarantee for future good behaviour. Members of the Home Guard who were formally captured wearing British Army uniforms were treated as POWs – armbands would not do, however.

Most of the resistance in this early period was simple vandalism of the 'tacks-on-the-road' variety, a minor irritant to the Germans. More serious were the activities of the Auxiliary Units, specially selected small groups of British troops who deliberately let themselves be overrun in order to conduct a guerrilla campaign behind enemy lines. Making good use of their local knowledge and operating from well-stocked and carefully concealed hide-outs, they proved a thorn in the side of the German military administration.

The arrival of reinforcements boosted the morale of the battered British divisions holding the line against the Germans. Under General Thorne's overall command these troops would make a second attempt to eject the invader from English soil. The light tanks of the 2nd Armoured Division could do

Right Two young refugees displaced by the fighting in Kent and Sussex. By the end of summer tens of thousands of people would be on the move as a result of the German occupation.

Below British troops prepare to fire a 25mm Hotchkiss anti-tank gun, a lightweight weapon of French origin.

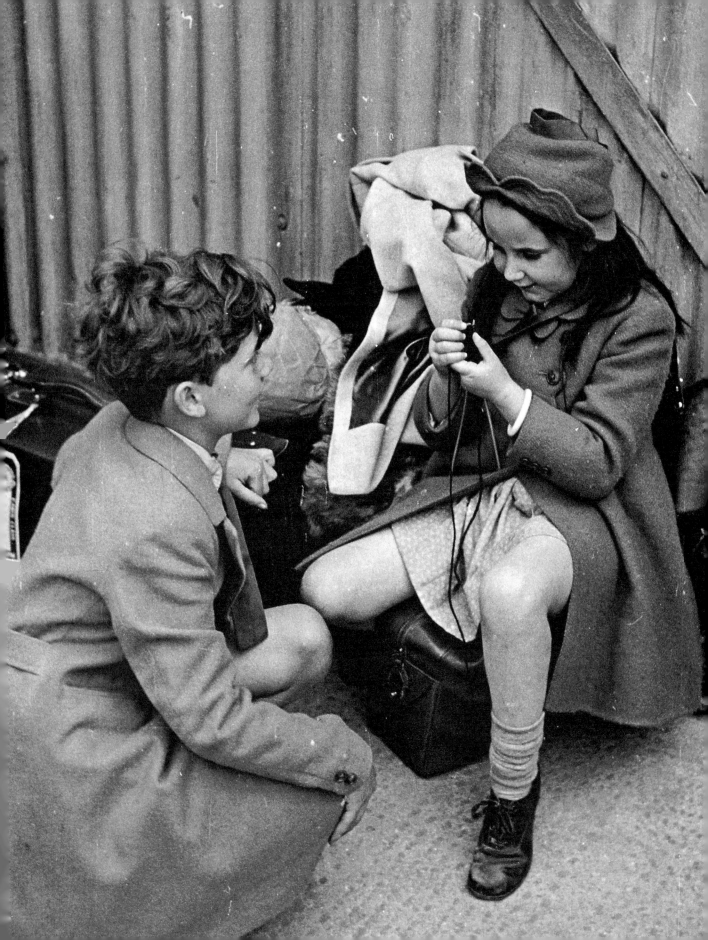

little against prepared German positions and the attack would once again be spearheaded by Matildas from the 1st Armoured Division, the light tanks following in support to exploit the anticipated breakthrough. Artillery and ammunition were still in short supply, but by carefully husbanding resources, a proper artillery barrage could be laid down to support the attack. Thorne's intention was to marshal his meagre forces for an all-or-nothing attack to cut through the enemy line near Ashford before racing for the coast to split their forces in two.

German aerial reconnaissance had noted the arrival of British reinforcements and Luftwaffe aircraft had harried them so effectively that the British were forced to conduct most troop movements during darkness. Despite this, Thorne camouflaged his intentions so successfully that when the attack went in at 6 am on 29 July the Germans were taken by surprise. The unexpected weight of British artillery fire and the sudden emergence of heavy tanks unnerved the Germans. Within a couple of hours a battalion of the 109th Infantry Regiment was encountered by its colonel falling back in disarray.

By midday a column of British tanks had advanced more than five miles and for once substantial groups of British infantry had kept up with them. For Major-General Hans Reinhard, commanding the 35th Infantry Division, it was a moment of crisis. This time the Luftwaffe had not been able to disrupt British movements, and the powerful 8.8cm dual-purpose guns had been bypassed by enemy tanks. At around 5 pm Matilda and Cruiser tanks were only a few miles from Reinhardt's HQ at Hythe.

Fortunately for the Germans, the arrival of reinforcements from Folkestone coincided with a loss of momentum in the British advance. Alongside a company of PzKpfw IIIs from the 3rd Panzer Division was the reconnaissance battalion of the SS Leibstandarte 'Adolf Hitler', whose troops raced into battle

Above left A column of British Cruiser Mk IV tanks advances across the heathland of Surrey in response to the invasion. Inadequately armoured and equipped with a feeble 2-pounder main armament, the Cruisers compared poorly with their German equivalents.

Left The advantage of air superiority: British transport vehicles lie destroyed by German dive bombers during an attempt to bring up reinforcements to the front line.

in armoured personnel carriers and armoured cars. While the German tanks attacked the British Matildas in the flank, the Leibstandarte troops leapfrogged them to deal with the infantry and light tanks.

The Leibstandarte had already gained a notorious reputation for brutality in Poland and France. The commander of the reconnaissance battalion was *SS Sturmbannführer* (Major) Kurt Meyer, a man driven by ruthless ambition. After smashing their way through a unit of light tanks from the 2nd Armoured Division, Meyer and his men were held up by Canadian troops staunchly holding their positions amid the wooded high ground of Wye Downs. Meyer was part of an advance guard pinned down by accurate machine-gun fire, and in his post-war account of the operation he described how he solved this tactical problem:

'We glue ourselves to the ground and dare not move. A feeling of nausea tightens in my throat. I yell to my men to get moving, but the man nearest me looks at me as if I am mad. Machine-gun fire smacks into the bushes beside us – how can I get them to make that first leap? In my despair, I feel the smoothness of an egg hand grenade in my hand. I shout at the group. Everybody looks thunderstruck as I brandish the hand grenade, pull the pin, and carefully roll it behind the last man in the group. Never again did I witness such a concerted leap forward as at that second. We race forward to a nearby ditch. The spell is broken. The hand grenade has cured our lameness. We grin at each other, and head forward towards the next cover.'

The fighting continued until after nightfall but the spirited German attack proved too much for the British, and as further German reserves were sent in, so the British were forced back. Both their armoured divisions were virtually destroyed and heavy casualties inflicted on the infantry. The next day the two armoured divisions were left with just 11 Heavy, 24 Cruiser and 41 Light tanks. Shortly before midnight on 29 July, Thorne rang Brooke to inform him of the failure. Reluctantly they agreed to pull back to the more defensible GHQ Line in order to better resist the expected German offensive. On 30 July British troops began to quietly disengage from their forward positions. The retreat had begun.

Although the German breakout had not been scheduled until 3 August, patrols had noted little or no resistance to their probings on 30 July. When this information reached Busch and his corps commanders they all agreed that this was a chance not to be missed. The attack must be launched immediately to prevent the British from establishing themselves further back. Accordingly the breakout was brought forward to first light on 1 August.

The basic German plan had already been decided: a two-pronged panzer assault would sweep west around London. Reinhardt's Panzer Group, too cumbersome to act as a single entity, was to split into two corps: XXXXI (assigned to the experienced tank commander General Herman Hoth) and the XV (formerly Hoth's Corps, but now given to 7th Panzer Division's commander and Hitler favourite, Lieutenant-General Erwin Rommel). The northern 'prong' – comprising XXXXI Panzer Corps (3rd and 10th Panzer Divisions, 'Grossdeutschland') – was to advance directly up the A20 road towards Maidstone, break through the GHQ Line and roll up British positions along the North Downs until west of Guildford before swinging due north to cross the Thames at Windsor. The southern 'prong' – XVth Corps (7th Panzer and 29th Motorized Divisions, Leibstandarte 'Adolf Hitler') – was to strike due west, roughly parallel with the south coast, securing Newhaven, Brighton and, most crucially, Portsmouth before turning northwards to support XXXXI Corps in outflanking London from the west. Meanwhile, the infantry formations of the First Wave would follow the panzers to deal with isolated strong points and then provide garrisons for the occupied territory.

In the Channel, the German Navy would supervise the transport of the Third Wave, a combination of between 11 and 14 panzer and infantry divisions, to complete the invasion. The Luftwaffe would continue to contain any RAF opposition, support the ground forces and safeguard the Channel supply line. That the German offensive was sprung prematurely was of little account to the overall success of the operation. Those supplies, weapons and troops which had not arrived on 1 August were rushed forward without much difficulty.

The two armies facing each other across the Kent–Sussex countryside were a generation apart; the superbly co-ordinated all-arms panzer divisions ran rings around the slow-moving masses of British infantry. Like the German breakthrough over the Meuse in May 1940, this offensive took the form of a race between each division for the furthest objective.

Without effective aerial reconnaissance, the

Above Senior officers of the Leibstandarte 'Adolf Hitler' discuss the progress of their regiment as refugees make their way down a country lane in Sussex. Dietrich stands in the centre of the group with Meyer (bareheaded) to his left. Meyer would go on to become the youngest divisional commander in the Wehrmacht.

British had only a vague idea of the build-up of German forces in England, and anyway lacked the forces to stop a major offensive regardless of where it came from. The first German tanks rolled over the start line at 4.30 am 1 August, supported by adequate artillery and Luftwaffe Stukas. XXXXI Corps, followed the retreating British rearguards with ease. After six hours tanks of the 10th Panzer Division reached the outskirts of Maidstone; by the end of the day the GHQ Line had been breached. The next day

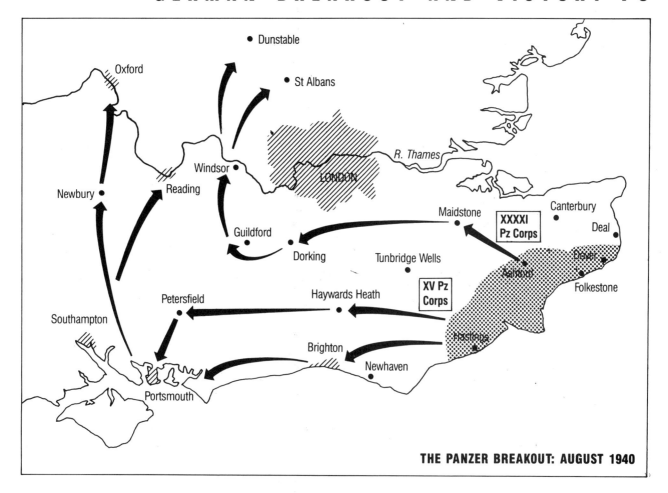

THE PANZER BREAKOUT: AUGUST 1940

a series of British stop-lines were either broken or bypassed, as the German panzers advanced remorselessly along the A25. By nightfall Sevenoaks, Limpsfield, Reigate and Dorking had fallen to the XXXXI Corps. No attempt was made to follow British troops retreating towards London; the dangers of protracted street fighting in the world's largest city were justifiably feared by the panzer commanders.

The XV Panzer Corps had got off to a slower start, held up by unexpected resistance around Heathfield. Once this had been overcome, the Germans found themselves facing the Canadians dug-in around Haywards Heath. The Leibstandarte 'Adolf Hitler' suffered heavy casualties at the hands of their old Canadian opponents. Three assaults were beaten back and the regimental commander spent two uncomfortable hours immobilized in No Man's Land while the battle raged around him. Eventually the Canadians were forced to retreat but, enraged by their losses, some Leibstandarte troops (with Meyer's full knowledge) shot a group of Canadian prisoners.

This act provoked a new ferocity between the two combatants.

Once the initial resistance had been overcome, the Germans surged ahead. Rommel pushed his troops relentlessly. Supported by the 1st Mountain Division, the 29th Motorized Division moved along the coast, capturing Newhaven and Brighton, reaching Chichester by late afternoon on 2 August. From Haywards Heath the 7th Panzer Division, with a depleted Leibstandarte in tow, raced along the A272 to Petersfield before swinging south towards Portsmouth. There the panzers halted, fearful of being involved in street fighting. Although the PzKpfw IVs, armed with 7.5cm guns, provided a degree of artillery support, it was left to the infantry to deal with the town's stubborn garrison.

Using inflatable boats, elements of the 29th Motorized Division bypassed Hayling Island to attack Portsmouth, while the Leibstandarte and the infantry of the 7th Panzer Division fought their way through the town from the north. The destroyers of the Ports-

mouth Flotilla were forced to withdraw while the garrison (now comprising Royal Marines and the remnants of a battalion of the Somerset Light Infantry), fought on until last light on 3 August.

As the German mechanized formations moved westward, the infantry divisions of the First Wave followed. The XIII Corps secured the rest of Kent: 17th Infantry Division advanced north to take Deal, Canterbury and the Isle of Thanet; 22nd Air Landing Division followed the panzers of XXXXI Corps, mopping up northern Kent before setting up a cordon around the south of London in an arc from Dartford to Epsom. The 1st Mountain Division was committed to a breathless chase behind the 29th Motorized Division while the 35th Infantry Division advanced between the two panzer corps along the Weald, securing Tunbridge Wells, East Grinstead and Crawley. The 7th Air and 7th Infantry Divisions (a cause of some confusion to later historians) remained as Sixteenth Army reserve, the paratroops being reassembled to act as another airborne force should the need arise.

The XXXXI Panzer Corps spent 3 August consolidating its position. Remaining pockets of British resistance were dealt with while reinforcements of men, ammunition and equipment were rushed forward. The British GHQ Line had been broken by

Above A Messerschmitt Bf 109 is refuelled using local transport at Hawkinge airfield, 2 August 1940. The use of British airfields allowed the Luftwaffe to provide effective support for ground operations throughout southern England.

Above right Lieutenant-General Erwin Rommel, newly promoted commander of XV Panzer Corps, consults with his staff officers as the offensive begins.

Right A Fiesler Storch reconnaissance plane flies over a tank company of the 7th Panzer Division as it rests in a valley on the Hampshire Downs.

the violence of XXXXI Corps' attack but many regular units of the British Army stood firm. On 4 August, as the Germans moved around London, they were stopped dead by two of the best British infantry divisions committed to the battle – Major-General N. M. S. Irwin's 2nd and Major-General B. L. Montgomery's 3rd Infantry Divisions. Still in the lead the German 10th Panzer Division was all but finished as a combat formation when Montgomery's artillery caught it advancing towards the Hog's Back, west of Guildford. The 3rd Panzer Division, however, eventually broke through Irwin's lines between

Leatherhead and Guildford, forcing both British formations to withdraw in order to avoid being cut off.

On 5 August the 'Grossdeutschland' and 3rd Panzer Division raced each other for the honour of reaching the Thames first. A company of scouting PzKpfw IIs fired over the river at a surprised Home Guard unit near Oakley Green (in fact boys from nearby Eton College) but it was the troops of the 'Grossdeutschland' who established the first bridgehead over the Thames, within sight of the Royal Windsor castle. The demolition of several Thames bridges had been rendered impossible by the speed of the German advance. By 6 August German troops were driving into the Chilterns; soon they would be in a position to encircle London.

Further south in Hampshire, the Leibstandarte and ensuing infantry units were left to clear up while the 7th Panzer and 29th Motorized Divisions took up position on the left flank of the XXXXI Panzer Corps. On 5 August Reading and Newbury fell to the XV Corps. The following day Oxford was captured in an exceptionally audacious move by a unit of PzKpfw 38(t) tanks who caught the bewildered British completely off guard. The news of Oxford's fall evoked deep depression among the Chiefs-of-Staff and the British cabinet. For the first time serious talk of peace was heard in Westminster and Whitehall. The British people were stunned by the collapse of their armed forces and the old determination to carry on the fight was now being eroded by a rising bitterness against the Government.

General Busch's elation at the rapidity of his Army's progress was matched by a sober assessment of recent losses. Not only had the British inflicted casualties on all formations (some very heavy), the distance of the advance had left a trail of broken-down tanks along the roads of southern England. By the evening of 6 August the three panzer divisions were at half-strength and the motorized units had suffered similar losses. The Luftwaffe too was struggling; besides continuing casualties in the air, more aircraft were being lost in support of ground forces and in battles with the Royal Navy. Never had the Luftwaffe been so stretched and Göring mused to Kesselring that if this loss rate continued there would be no Air Force at all within two weeks.

However, the capture of Southampton docks virtually intact and the speedy reopening of the harbour at Portsmouth allowed the steady transhipment of the Third Wave, a further seven infantry and two panzer divisions of Colonel-General Adolf Strauss's Ninth Army. Against such odds Britain had no hope.

Once again Hitler and his astute propaganda chief Dr Josef Goebbels publicly offered a 'generous settlement'. With over 200,000 German soldiers on British soil, they were greeted with less contempt than before. On the morning of 7 August, at an emergency meeting of the CIGS and the full British Cabinet, Churchill was forced to concede that the military situation was grave in the extreme. Appeals to the Americans had failed to yield concrete results; alone the British armed forces were bound to be defeated.

During this famous conference, the debate ranged from immediate surrender to carrying on the war indefinitely, the Government going underground if necessary. Eventually it was decided that the armed forces would have to surrender, but the Royal Family and key Cabinet members should be spirited out of the country to carry on the fight from the Commonwealth. At least the Fleet was largely intact and perhaps one day it would act as the springboard for a return. At first Churchill, along with other defiant members, refused to accept the idea of fleeing the country, but eventually they were forced to accept that their vision of going out in a blaze of glory would more likely end in an ignominious capture by the Germans, their fate a useful bargaining tool for the Nazis.

As a safeguard, Britain's gold reserves and securities had already been shipped to Canada, and preparations for the departure of the Royal Family had been made. Once the British Government had made its decision, there was no time to lose. While the German spearheads fought their way along the Chilterns towards St Albans and Dunstable, two secret trains left London for the battlecruiser *Renown*, anchored off Liverpool. In a moment of supreme tragedy, King George VI and Churchill stood on the deck as the warship slipped her cables, watched in

Above right The view from a Czech-built PzKpfw 35(t) during the Blitzkrieg through southern England. The swastika flags draped over the engine decks of the tanks acted as a means of identification for the Luftwaffe.
Right Advancing from the playing fields of Eton, the School's Home Guard unit prepares to do battle with the Germans, 4 August. The following day the Eton schoolboys were badly cut up by machine-gun fire from a German panzer unit at Oakley Green.

silence by a small, dispirited group of onlookers.

On 7 August the rump of the British Government contacted the Swedish ambassador to request an armistice with the Germans. On hearing the British offer, Hitler and the German High Command were overjoyed. Hitler's greatest gamble had paid off. At 6 pm on 8 August hostilities ceased and the next morning representatives of the newly promoted Field Marshal Busch motored through the streets of London to Whitehall. For the first time since 1066, a foreign military power had successfully invaded Britain. The country now lay at Germany's mercy.

Top British volunteers help clear up the debris in Haywards Heath in the aftermath of the German attack of 2 August.

Above German assault troops take cover in the face of a British artillery bombardment near Petersfield.

Above right A junior German infantry officer explains the results of a reconnaissance mission to his company commander. As the panzer advance gained momentum, so the infantry found it an increasing problem keeping up with the mechanised units.

Right Despite occasional atrocities, relations between the two armies were generally good. A German medic gives first aid to a British soldier wounded in the fighting around Reading, 5 August.

THE GERMAN OCCUPATION

As the British and German representatives sat down to discuss surrender terms, German mechanized units advanced into the Midlands and North of England. Birmingham was formally occupied on 10 August and Liverpool, Manchester, Sheffield and Leeds also fell during the ensuing six days. A few British units – mainly those that had not seen action – refused to keep the armistice ceasefire. Scattered across the country, they were unable to put up any effective resistance and were easily overrun. Furthermore, the punitive destruction of Litchfield and Grantham discouraged further last stands. ___

By the end of August, German troops were stationed in the main urban centres and other key positions in England and Wales. In Northern Ireland and Scotland, advance parties had arrived in Belfast, Glasgow and Edinburgh. Field Marshal Busch and his HQ took up residence in the Horse Guards, the rest of Whitehall being occupied by the other various German ministries in the course of time. For Admiral Karl Dönitz, deputy chief of the Kriegsmarine and prisoner of the British during the previous war, to pass under Admiralty Arch was certainly a moment to savour. The German labour leader, Dr Robert Ley was another of the visiting dignitaries to be seen strutting around the sights of London in the heady days just after the Wehrmacht's great victory. On a more purely practical note, the shipment of Field Marshal Walther von Reichenau's Sixth Army through the ports of Southampton and Portsmouth brought total German strength in Britain to over 750,000 men. Reichenau – one of Hitler's 'Nazi generals' – was appointed Military Governor of the United Kingdom, a position he held until his death in December 1942 through a heart attack.

Against this background of a remorseless German war machine taking over the country, the British had little option but to agree to the surrender terms. The Germans, however, were furious that they were unable to negotiate with the British Government proper. Their chagrin was increased by the successful departure of the Royal Navy (with many ocean-going merchant vessels) from Home waters. In addition, the British representatives steadfastly refused to accept responsibility for any overseas possessions; they had been empowered to accept surrender terms for the United Kingdom alone, and German threats would not move them from this position.

By the terms of the agreement signed on 18

Right A German military band marches through the streets of Tunbridge Wells, part of Field Marshal Walther von Richenau's Sixth Army. Throughout August and September the streets in the towns of southern England reverberated to the tramp of hundreds of thousands of German soldiers, advancing to take up their positions as Britain's Army of Occupation.

August, the British Government (national and local) was to work alongside and under the command of the Germans. The other important clause was the surrender of all British troops. Needless to say, the surrender order was not universally obeyed and between 40,000 and 50,000 men slipped away in the confusion. Some of these were able to get overseas; others went underground.

The British Government-in-Exile (as it called itself) had been immediately outlawed by the Germans. This comprised the Royal Family, the Prime Minister and certain members of the war cabinet. Protected by the Royal Navy, they had all arrived

WANTED

FOR INCITEMENT TO

MURDER

Above A poster issued by the Nazi authorities in the immediate aftermath of the official surrender, and following Churchill's flight into exile.

Above left One of the many long lines of British soldiers seen making their way into captivity during the autumn of 1940.

Left A group of veteran German infantry take a breather on a route march between Sheffield and Leeds.

safely in Canada, but for political reasons it was decided that they should find a more permanent haven in the Bahamas.

The bulk of the British Fleet was based in Canada and most British refugees fled to this country, or the USA. Calling themselves the Free British, they were now one of the many exile movements in the New World. Until America's entry into the war in February 1942, this was an extremely difficult time for them, consigned to a new and painful position as mere observers on the sidelines of the world stage. The days of imperial grandeur were over, the British reduced to the role of supplicant to the USA and the old Commonwealth and Empire.

In Britain the Germans installed a two-tier administration: the Army at the top, issuing orders to be carried out by the British civil administration. An immediate problem for the Germans was to find suitable Britons to form a new governing body. Early hopes of enlisting the most famous pro-fascist British politician, Sir Oswald Mosley, were dashed. Mosley, only recently freed from Brixton Prison where he had been held by the Churchill Government, refused to have any direct dealings with the Germans unless they withdrew their armies from British soil.

After this initial rebuff, the German military authorities turned to Sir Samuel Hoare, a former Foreign Secretary, whose pro-appeasement views had forced him from office before the war. Hoare had been sent as British Ambassador to Franco's Spain and after discussions with senior members of the German Foreign Office, he accepted their offer to return to Britain as leader of the British National Council, a new organization set up by Germans – in effect to rubber stamp their administrative decisions. The Germans also succeeded in securing the services of the renowned military theorist, historian and retired soldier Major-General J. F. C. Fuller to act as Hoare's deputy.

Other members of the Council were minor public figures: old cronies of the German Foreign Minister and former Ambassador to St James, Joachim von Ribbentrop; disgruntled civil servants and passed-over ex-soldiers; and the usual quota of right-wing fanatics. Perphaps in fairness to some of the Council members, it should be pointed out that they felt a genuine sense of responsibility towards the country. Politically naive, they at least considered that their very presence would act as a buffer between the Germans and the British people.

The high-level German discussions with Hoare

in Madrid had included the delicate subject of a possible return for the Duke of Windsor. Hoare was quick to see the advantages to his administration of support from such an illustrious source, while the Duke was easily persuaded that his country needed him in 'this moment of destiny'.

Rather than reassuming his old title of King Edward VIII – the fact that his brother had been crowned George VI made the whole idea a constitutional minefield – the Duke of Windsor retained his present title, but was accorded the rank of Regent. The German authorities scored a major propaganda triumph with their carefully stage-managed ceremony to greet the arrival of the Duke and Duchess. Cameras rolled and military bands played as Field Marshal Reichenau officially welcomed them back to Britain when they landed at Croydon Aerodrome.

The Germans were pleased with their work in setting up a broadly compliant British civil administration. Despite the platitudes regarding Anglo-German unity, the British position in this relationship was to be almost totally subservient. Indeed, under the brutal (though secret) dictates of Field Marshal von Brauchitsch's *Orders concerning the Organization and Function of Military Government in*

Top The deportations begin: a group of supporters of the New Left Book Club are led away to a transit camp in the Midlands, April 1941. Initially, these round-ups were thought to be only temporary and were not taken that seriously, but as the months and years went by the sinister nature of the occupation became only too apparent.

Above Sir Samuel Hoare (centre), leader of the British National Council.

England (9 September 1940), Britain was to be cowed into submission and stripped bare. Although not all the points of the *Function of Military Government* were put into full and immediate effect – notably the economically self-defeating point 4 – Brauchitsch's orders were to form much of the basis of German policy towards Britain. For this reason, the key sections are quoted at length:

'Most Secret: Directive for Military Government in England.
1 The main task of military government is to make full use of the country's resources for the needs of the fighting troops and the requirements of the German war economy.
2 An essential condition for securing the labour of the country is that law and order should prevail. Law and order will therefore be established. Administrative measures will not violate international law unless the Army has given cause for reprisals.
3 Armed insurgents of either sex will be dealt with the utmost severity. If the population initiates active operations, the inhabitants involved in the fighting will be regarded as armed insurgents. When taking hostages, those persons should, if

Top While a British policeman looks on, Luftwaffe troops march through Hyde Park as part of the German victory celebrations.

Above The German propaganda minister, Dr Joseph Goebbels was one of the many top Nazis who visited London. During his visit in March 1941 he was the official guest of the Regent, Edward Duke of Windsor. Both men got on well, as can be seen from this photograph taken in Buckingham Palace.

possible, be selected in whom the *active* enemy elements have an interest.

4 The able-bodied male population between the ages of 17 and 45 will, unless the local situation calls for an exceptional ruling, be interned and despatched to the mainland with a minimum of delay.

5 Local headquarters and unit commanders are forbidden to raise levies or other monetary taxes.

32

30. **Catlin**, geb. **Brittain**, Vera, Journalistin, London SW 3, 19 Glebe Place, RSHA VI G 1.
31. **Cazalet**, Victor Alexander, 27.12.96, Offizier, London W 1, 66 Grosvenor Street, RSHA VI G 1.
32. **Cebular**, Alfred, zuletzt: Novi Sad, vermutl. England, RSHA IV F 4.
33. **Cecil**, Lord, Robert, geb. 1864, London, 16 South Eaton Place, RSHA VI G 1.
34. **Le Cerep**, Frederik, 22.3.96 New York, Advokat, England (Kraftw. AMO 269 GB), RSHA IV E 4.
35. **Chain**, Ernst, Dr., 1906, zuletzt Oxford, RSHA III A 1.
36. **Chaloner**, Thomas, 18.8.99 Wiltshire, brit. Cpt., England, RSHA IV E 4.
37. **Chamberlain** (Arthur) Neville, 18.3.69, Politiker, ehemaliger Ministerpräsident, London S. W. 1, 10 Downing-Street, Westbourne, Edgaston, Birmingham, RSHA II D 5 — VI G 1.
38. **Chamier**, Fred William, 8.4.76 Stanmore b. Sydney, Dr. d. Staatswissenschaft, England, RSHA IV E 4.
39. **Chapman**, Sir. Sidney John, 29.1.88, Prof., London S. W. 7, The Imperial College, RSHA VI G 1.
40. **Charles**, B., brit. Agentin, zuletzt: Brüssel, vermutl. England (Täterkreis: Josef Menneken), RSHA IV E 4.
41. **Charoux** geborene Treibl, Margarete, 26.5.95, Wien, Reisende, London, RSHA IV A 1.
42. **Charoux**, Siegfried, 15.10.96 Wien, Bildhauer, London W. 4, Riverside 51, British Grove, RSHA IV A 1, III A.
43. **Chidson**, M. Reamy, 13.4.98 London, Militärattaché, brit. Oberstleutn. zuletzt: Den Haag, vermutl. England (Kraftw.: HZ 86 987 GB.), RSHA IV E 4.
43a. **China**, John, Edwin, 21.1.01 Dradlington, zuletzt: Kopenhagen, vermutl. England, RSHA IV E 4.
44. **Chingford**, Charles, Vertreter, London W.d, Cambridge 119, RSHA IV E 4.
45. **Choustzarias**, Andreas, Arzt, zuletzt Athen, vermutl. England (Täterkreis: Crawford), RSHA IV E 4.
46. **Choiseul-Gouffier**, Louis, zuletzt: Kowno, vermutl. England (Täterkreis: Th. Camber), RSHA IV E 4, Stapo Tilsit.
47. **Chrisosten**, Segrue John, 7.1.84, Liverpool, Journalist, England, RSHA IV E 4.
47a. **Christie**, brit. Nachrichtenoffizier, London, RSHA IV E 4.
48. **Church**, Archibald George, 1886 London, Major, Rostrevor, Seledos-Road, Sanderstreet, RSHA VI G 1.
49. **Churchill**, Winston Spencer, Ministerpräsident, Westerham/Kent, Chartwell Manor, RSHA VI A 1.
50. **Chwatal**, Johann, 16.8.92 Suchenthal, vermutl. England, RSHA IV A 1.
51. **Chwatal**, Silvester, 21.11.94 Suchenthal, vermutl. England, RSHA IV A 1.
52. **Cibulak**, Gerhard, 12.11.08 Barnim, London N. W. 2, 47 Blenheim Gardens, RSHA IV A 1.
53. **Cichy**, Georg, 30.9.14 Scharley/Ostoberschlesien, Obergefreiter, vermutl. England, RSHA IV E 5, Stapo Oppeln.
54. **Cigna**, Vladimir, 3.6.98 Olmütz, ehem. tschech. Stabsopt., London 53 Lexan Gardens, Kensington W. 8 (Täterkreis: Frantisek-Moravec), RSHA IV E 4, IV E 6.

Above A page from the SS 'Special Search List GB', a publication issued by the RSHA to track down opponents of the Nazi system. Included here are the two former prime ministers, Chamberlain and Churchill and the journalist Vera Brittain.
Right Members of the British Union of Fascists take the salute from a German infantry regiment.

- 67 -

Gesundheitspolizei.

Sanitary Police.

- - - - - - - - - - - - - - - - - - - -

Ansteckende Krankheiten.

Die Massnahmen der öffentlichen Gesundheits- und Reinlichkeitspflege sind von höchster Bedeutung für die Sicherheit der Besatzungstruppen und daher genauestens zu beachten.

Jeder Fall einer übertragbaren oder ansteckenden Krankheit ist sofort von der örtlichen Zivilbehörde zur Kenntnis der in dem betreffenden Ort befindlicher Militärbehörde zu bringen.

Der Militärbefehlshaber kann Offiziere besonders beauftragen die Durchführung der gesundheitspolizeilichen Massnahmen durch die zuständigen Zivilbehörden zu kontrolieren, besonders hinsichtlich der Prostitution und der Verhütung von Geschlechtskrankheiten. Diese Offiziere haben ausserdem dafür zu sorgen, dass seitens der Zivilbehörden keine Massnahmen ergriffen werden, die in ihrer Folge das Ansehen oder die Sicherheit der Besatzungstruppen schädigen.

Prostitution.

Die Gerichtsbarkeit gegen sich umhertreibende Frauen wird durch die Polizeigerichte der deutschen Truppen im besetzten Gebiet ausgeübt.

Eine Frau, die sich umhertreibt ist im Sinne dieser Verordnung:
a) jede Frau, deren gewöhnlicher Aufenthaltsort ausserhalb der besetzten Zone liegt und sich in der Zone ohne nachweisbaren Unterhalt aufhält.
b) jede Frau, die unerlaubten Geschlechtsverkehr mit einer Person

Infectious Diseases.

Whereas the measures of health and sanitation are of greatest importance for the security of the troops of occupation strictest observance is necessary.

Every case of contagious or infectious disease shall immediately be reported by the Civil local Authorities to the Military Authority stationed in the locality.

The Military Commander may appoint officers specially to supervise the sanitary police regulations to be executed by the Civil Authorities, especially those relating to prostitution and the prevention of venereal disease. These officers shall also see that the measures taken by the Civil Authorities are not designed to prejudice, and do not in practice affect, the dignity or the safety of the troops of occupation.

Prostitution.

The Provost Courts of the German troops in the occupied territory shall exercise jurisdiction concerning vagrant women.

A vagrant woman within the meaning of this order is:
a) any woman whose usual place of abode is outside the zone of occupation present therein without visible means of support.

b) any woman who solicits or has illicit sexual intercourse with

The authority for such measures is retained by the Army commander and the offices expressly empowered by him.

6 Laws of the country operative prior to the occupation will be upheld unless they are contradictory to the purposes of the occupation. English authorities may continue to function if they maintain a correct attitude.

7 Special attention is to be paid to public health affairs.

8 In the interests of the country's national economy, this being the concern of the Defence Economic Staff and its headquarters, the welfare of the inhabitants of the country will be considered in so far as they contribute directly or indirectly

Left and below Examples from the *Organization and Function of Military Government in England,* the framework for German rule in the United Kingdom. The German Army had long experience in acting as an occupying power, and these pages reveal the special attention paid to the dangers of espionage and the spread of infectious diseases.

Article 6.

No person shall sell any alcoholic beverage or intoxicating or stupifying drug to members of the troops of occupation in contravention of regulations issued by the armies. Upon a second conviction in such a case the court in addition to the ordinary penalties provided may order the closing of the establishment in which the offence was committed, for a period of not more than three months provided that the responsibility of the owner has been established.

Article 7.

All merchants, manufacturers and retailers, and, in general all persons trading with the public are forbidden to sell to any member of the German forces or to any German official any commodity or article of any sort whatsoever to a higher price than that paid by others.

Part IV.

Ordinance regarding Espionage.

Article 1.

If any person for any purpose prejudicial to the safety of the Army of Occupation
a) approaches, inspects, passes over or enters any place the access to which shall, by order duly published, be specially prohibited, with a view to the security of the Army of Occupation, by the Military Commander;
b) makes any photograph, sketch, plan, model, map, or note or other document;
c) obtains, collects, records, has in his possession, publishes or communicates to any other person any photograph, sketch, plan, model, map or note, or other document of information;
d) engages in a conspiracy or holds communication with powers other than those participating in the occupation;
he shall be liable to imprisonment for life or for such term as the court may determine.

Artikel 2.

Niemand darf ohne schriftliche Genehmigung des Oberbefehlshabers der Besetzungs-Zone einen Lichtbildapparat mit sich führen an Orten, deren Betreten verboten ist.
Niemand darf eine drahtlose Telegraphen- oder eine drahtlose Fernsprechstation errichten oder einen Sende- oder Empfangsapparat zu seiner Verfügung haben, ohne einen besonderen Ausweis vorlegen zu können.

Artikel 3.

Jede Person macht sich strafbar, die einen Reisepass oder Militärpass, einen Geleitschein, einen Erlaubnisschein oder irgend ein anderes Dokument fälscht oder verfälscht oder abändert oder wissentlich falsche Aussagen macht.

VERORDNUNG .

Bestandsaufnahme der Hilfsmittel für militärische Zwecke.

Es ist wichtig, dass die deutsche Wehrmacht die Hilfsmittel kennt, die sie in den besetzten Gebieten zu militärischen Zwecken benötigt.

Artikel 1.

In den besetzten Gebieten ist eine Bestandsaufnahme und Klasseneinteilung vorzunehmen bezüglich solcher Transportmittel wie Wagen, Automobile, Motorräder, Fahrräder, Pferde usw., wie bezüglich des Materials dieser Art, welches für militärische Zwecke geeignet ist: Fabriken, öffentliche oder private Unternehmungen, die zur Herstellung oder Ausbesserung von Heeresmaterial verwendet werden können, ferner bezüglich des zum Betriebe der etwa mit Beschlag zu belegenden Gegenstände nötigen Personals.

Artikel 2.

Die Bestandsaufnahme wird von den Zivilbehörden des besetzten Landes unter deren eigener Verantwortung ausgeführt.

towards the maintenance of law and order and the securing of the country's labour for the requirements of the troops and the German war economy.'

Under the aegis of the Military Economic Staff (*Wehrwirtschaftsstab England*) the United Kingdom was divided into six Military Economic Commands, with headquarters in London, Birmingham, Liverpool, Newcastle, Glasgow and Belfast (the latter moving south to Dublin after the direct military occupation of the Republic in 1942). Initially, these commands were concerned with the direct supply to German troops in Britain – notably fuel and basic provisions – but subsequently they turned their attention towards the economic exploitation of Britain in the interests of the German war machine.

Deportations were largely confined to prisoners of war, and those labelled by the Nazis as 'undesirables'. Some industries were dismantled, especially those concerns that posed a threat to home industries in Germany. Thus, for example, the great chemical works on the Tees were run down while on the outskirts of west London the famous Hoover factory was transformed into a supply depot for the German Army's London Command. For obvious practical reasons, heavy industry was left largely intact,

Below The notorious head of the RSHA, Reinhard Heydrich working at his desk. Himmler's right-hand man, Heydrich was responsible for the arrest, torture and death of countless thousands of innocent people. Appointed protector of Bohemia-Moravia he was assassinated by Czech partisans in 1942 (financed by the Czech Government in America). **Bottom** Amidst the destruction of the market town of Grantham, attempts are made to rescue valuables from the rubble.

Above On the outskirts of Bath, Wehrmacht troops discuss their route with a British motorcycle despatch rider. While London remained as the favoured posting for German troops, 'Baedeker' cities such as Bath were also popular, and there was fierce rivalry to secure appropriate positions.

Left A German Luftwaffe officer talks to a traffic policeman. The occupation placed the British police in an impossible position: ordered by the terms of the surrender agreement to work with the German authorities, when did co-operation end and outright collaboration begin?

Right Colonel Charles de Gaulle is led into the courtroom where he was tried by the Vichy Government and sentenced to death for treason. De Gaulle's fate was shared by several other exiled leaders who were caught by the Gestapo and shipped back to show trials in their own countries.

although operating at reduced capacity. German industrialists pressed for a more radical 'restructuring' of British industry but when preparations were set in motion for the invasion of the Soviet Union early in 1941, it was decided that it would be more effective to leave it *in situ* to work directly for Germany.

Alongside the Army was the Reich Central Security Office, or *Reichssicherheitshauptamt* (RSHA), a combination of the more repressive organizations under Nazi rule: the Gestapo (Secret State Police), Kripo (Criminal Police) and the SD or *Sicherheitsdienst* (Secret Service of the Party). Under Heydrich's direct control, the RSHA imposed its sway over the people of Britain. Even before the invasion had got underway, Heydrich had issued the following order to *SS Standartenführer* (Colonel) Professor Dr Six:

'. . . The *Reichsführer SS*'s [Himmler] Security Police and SD will commence their activities simultaneously with the military invasion in order to seize and combat effectively the numerous important organizations and societies in England which are hostile to Germany . . . Your task is to combat, with the requisite means, all anti-German organizations, institutions, opposition and opposition groups which can be seized in England, to prevent the removal of all available material, and to capitalize and safeguard it for future exploitation. I designate the capital, London, as the location for your headquarters as Representative of the Chief of the Security Police and SD; and I authorize you to set up small action groups (*Einsatzgruppen*) in other parts of Great Britain as the situation dictates and the necessity arises.'

The *Einsatzgruppen*, or 'action squads' operated from regional headquarters in London, Bristol, Birmingham, Liverpool, Manchester, Edinburgh and (after 1942) Dublin. Their role was to create a climate of terror to subdue the spirit of the general population. The RSHA had already published its *Die Sonderfahndungsliste GB* ('Special Search List GB') which consisted of over 2,700 names of prominent individuals with supplements of businesses, institutions and other organizations which the Nazis deemed worthy of close inspection.

The *Einsatzgruppen* were instructed not to delay in apprehending the names on the 'Special Search List', all of whom were to be closely interrogated. Despite this, almost a quarter of the names on the list escaped arrest, and were able to flee to safety of one sort or another. Of those taken into custody, over half were released as 'not constituting a threat to the Reich Government'. Among these were such luminaries as Virginia Woolf, Noel Coward and Lord and Lady Baden-Powell (although the Scout Movement was officially proscribed, its avowed international approach being anathema to the Nazis).

Others, such as the radical journalist Claude Cockburn, the politician Alfred Duff Cooper and the writer Vera Brittain were less fortunate and found themselves herded into cattle-trucks bound for Germany. The Gestapo reserved special venom for the many exiles living in Britain, most of whom were ardently anti-Nazi. Probably the most famous of these was the leader of the Free French, Charles de Gaulle; his fate was to be returned to the jurisdiction of Vichy France and a firing squad. Alongside the various socialists and other obvious opponents of Nazi Germany, the main target of the *Einsatzgruppen* was, of course, the Jewish community.

The various elements of the RSHA achieved considerable success in gaining a strong measure of control over the British people in the post-invasion months. This was partly due to their own skill and ruthlessness in dealing with subject peoples, but they also received help from the British authorities. The police force had little option but to co-operate with its new masters, but they also played an important role in acting as a barrier – no matter how ineffective – between the roving bands of *Einsatzgruppen* and the civil population. Frequently, British policemen tipped off local individuals they knew were about to be raided. On the other hand, however, the police were often less than partial when it came to those who were considered a 'nuisance' for one reason or another – mainly communists and foreign exiles. In time this led to the killings of certain over-zealous policemen and other selected members of the 'Administration of England'. On all sides, the occupation was a time when scores were settled, often permanently.

Above right Field Marshal Gerd von Rundstedt (C-in-C of Army Group A) congratulates a unit from the 7th Infantry Division.

Right A cinema in Swansea is converted for a showing of the German propaganda epic, 'Victory in the West'.

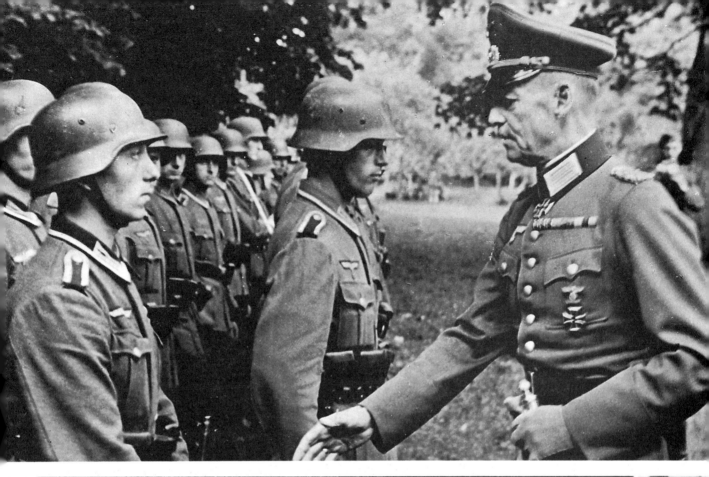

GAUMONT PALACE

AIR RAID SHELTER

AIR RAID SHELTER

Sieg im Westen

GAUMONT PALACE PRESENTS

Sieg im Westen

BRITAIN UNDER THE NAZI YOKE

The British response to the sudden and dramatic German takeover was essentially one of confusion and depression. For a proud and independent people, occupation was a humiliating blow. The loss of freedom, the very idea of the German jackboot tramping across 'England's Green and Pleasant Land' seemed unbearable. Yet bear it they must. The First World War images of the 'Beastly Hun', raping and pillaging his way across the country, were largely incorrect. The reality was both better and worse. The level of discipline maintained by the German armed forces was generally high, as the British were reluctantly forced to admit. But the extraordinary degree to which the vast totalitarian apparatus descended upon the country came as a terrible blow, affecting the lives of the population at almost every level.

Once the immediate shock of German occupation was over, however, the attitude of the majority of the population ranged from apathy to sullen resentment. Despite Churchill's encouragement to 'take one with you' (rendered increasingly irrelevant by his own departure) the British Government had not asked the people to rise up against the Germans. And life had to go on. The industrial workforce still went to its factories and other places of work; shopkeepers and other tradesmen carried on as best they could; the professions went about their business. Once the strangeness of the Germans had been overcome, people found to their surprise that they could be human too. Slowly, a relationship of sorts began to develop between the British people and members of the German armed forces and elements of the German civil administration. At the first Christmas of occupation, German garrisons made gifts of food and drink to the local communities – and many a child in hospital was given presents by a Father Christmas with an unfamiliar accent. These niceties were not to last, however, and, of course, never included any German who belonged to the RSHA or any other similar organization. Such individuals were feared and loathed in equal measure.

Operating outside and beyond the limits of occupied society, the Auxiliary units fought on, ignoring the ceasefire to become the first focus of British resistance. Some managed to carry on the battle until early in the new year but eventually all were located and put out of action. Those men who escaped capture, however, formed a valuable repository of military skills for later use.

Right A London bus is swallowed up by a bomb crater following a German raid, 4 August 1940. Although London was not heavily bombed by the Luftwaffe, damage such as this was a salutary reminder to the population at large of the devastating power of the German armed forces.

Above The underground execution cellar at Gestapo headquarters in Chiswick. A converted TA rifle range, the state of the wooden posts provides ample evidence of the numbers who met their deaths here.

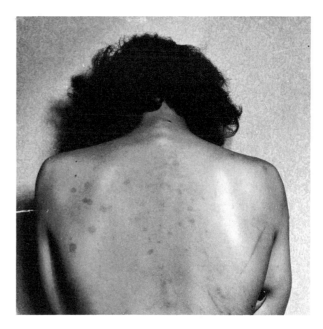

Above Torture was a basic weapon of the Gestapo; the cigarette burn scars on this member of the resistance are clearly visible, the result of interrogations following the killing of Rudolf Thyrolf.

The first six months after the invasion saw spontaneous acts of resistance from small groups or individuals unable to bear the shame and misery of occupation. Although such acts functioned as morale boosters for some, the Germans dealt with these relatively minor inconveniences with customary brutality. Many individuals were caught in the very act of opposition, while the amateur resistance groups of this early period were usually rounded up with disheartening swiftness. Once in the hands of the Gestapo, their fate was sealed. The German intelligence agencies used local police stations and the best hotels for their purposes. Both operated as centres for interrogation, where resistance members were tortured, and then executed once their usefulness had ended.

The daring assassination of *SS Sturmbannführer* (Major) Rudolf Thyrolf, deputy leader of the Liverpool *Einsatzgruppen*, outside his offices in the Liver Building on 3 February 1941 brought dire retribution. Thyrolf had been gunned down by a student from the university; under the torture he revealed the whereabouts of the rest of his 'terror-gang' – a mixed group of fellow students and dockers from the Port of Liverpool. While they were being rounded up. Heydrich had already telexed *SS Standartenführer* Six that an example must be set. The hostage execution ratio was increased twentyfold, from the standard 10 for each German killed to 200:1. Half were gunned down at the Goodison Park football ground, the remainder at Anfield. The collective punishment for the people of Liverpool was the withdrawal of fuel and the halving of basic food rations for three months (a decision which resulted in far more deaths than the executions). Inevitably, incidents like this caused mixed reactions: hatred of the Germans was almost universal in the city – from now on only the most desperate prostitute would have dealings with a German – but this was matched by the fearful reluctance of many to actively support the resistance.

The Thyrolf assassination was followed by several spectacular German counter-intelligence coups, leading to the public execution of many resistance leaders. During this stage of the occupation, the Gestapo and SD were helped by the ineptness of the

resistance groups, but they also received aid from certain sections of British intelligence, which were only too keen to throw in their lot with the Germans. These people, along with other 'co-operationists', had decided that Britain's future lay in the Europe of the New Order. Most effective was the information provided by MI5's F Branch which provided German security with an extensive catalogue of names and organizations to add to their own 'Search List'. Of course, other members of the British security services would have nothing to do with the Germans and covertly resisted them, but the damage had been done.

The surviving members of the British resistance accordingly changed tactics. From now on internal security was paramount and during 1941–4 the movement steered itself away from showy exploits. New policies included limited industrial disruption – often literally a spanner in the works – and the development of alternative information services. The latter were designed to build up networks of part-time volunteers who would be able to take up a more active role when the time came. Gradually the heavy bravado

Above A round up of hostages from an English village, sometime in the summer of 1943. Their fate was dependent on the behaviour of the local population; any 'outrages' would lead to automatic deportation or even execution.

of 1940 was replaced by a determined professionalism. As one writer of the conflict remarked, 'The Underground went underground'.

The old English liberties – real and imaginary – had been destroyed at a stroke by the German occupation. Simple identity cards were replaced by a series of documents which had to be renewed every six months. To be caught without satisfactory documentation was a serious offence, punishable by an automatic prison sentence of anything from three to 12 months. The English (and Scottish) legal systems remained, but under German military supervision. Crimes against German Army personnel or property were dealt with directly by military courts,

Whether the explosion of the gas main by Bank Underground Station on 11 November 1941 was an accident or sabotage was never satisfactorily ascertained, but the Germans decided on the latter and shot 20 hostages in the Tower of London.

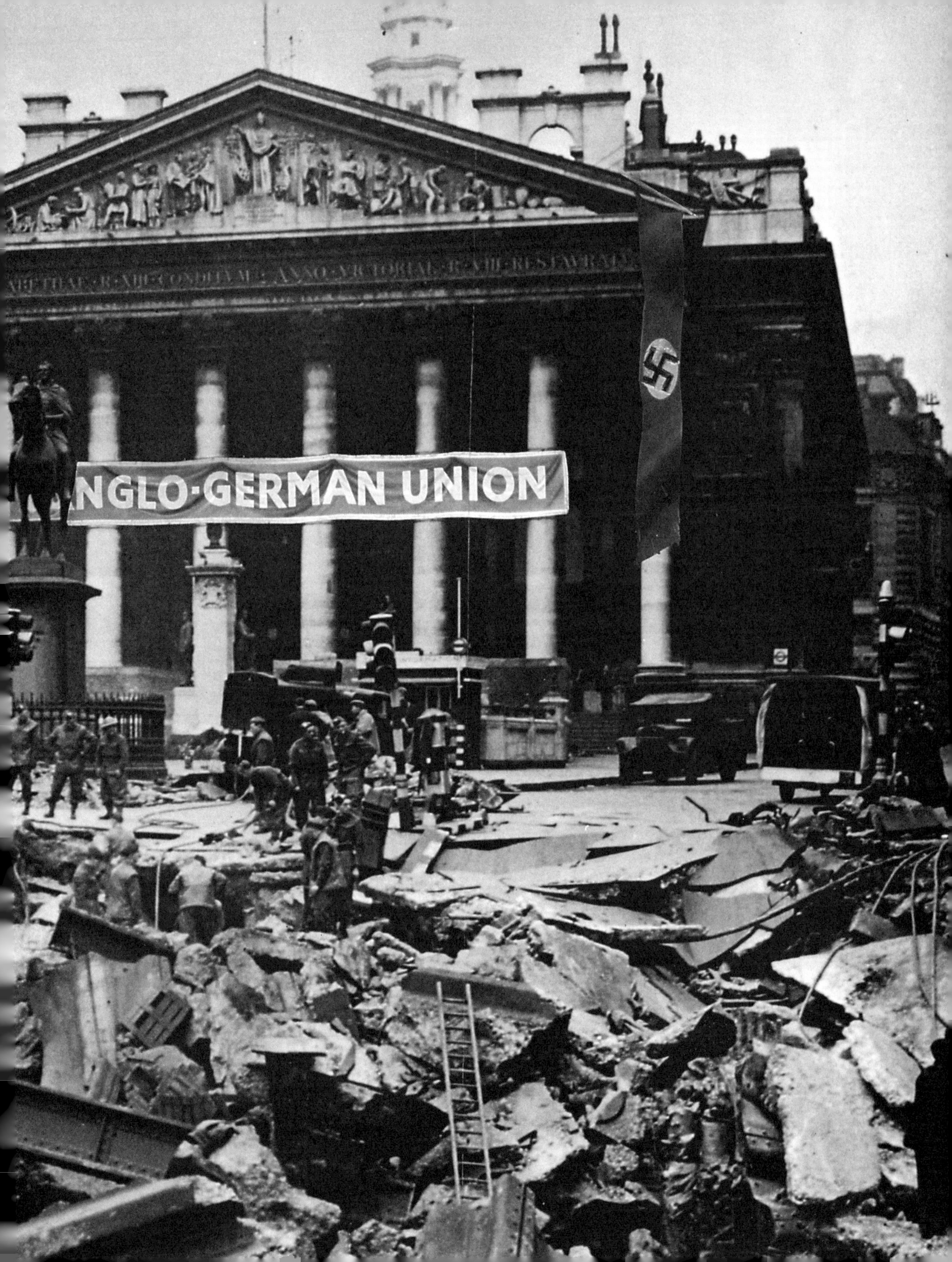
NGLO-GERMAN UNION

while 'crimes against the state' fell within the jurisdiction of the RSHA.

Censorship was imposed with iron rigidity. Any newspaper or magazine editor was liable for imprisonment for the most minor infractions of the censorship code. For over a year the *Daily Telegraph* carefully placed all official German announcements in its 'Fifth Column'; the censor's 'discovery' led to 18 months in Guildford Camp for the editor and a month's suspension for the paper. More serious offences led to the outright closure of the publication. Paper shortages during 1944 were so drastic, however, that most titles began to disappear altogether, and the few that survived consisted of little more than a folded broadsheet.

Some newspapers, by contrast, went abroad,

Right A typically posed resistance photograph shows the preparation of an underground news-sheet in Glasgow, 1943–4. The pistols are purely for show.

Below A captured resistance group are lined up for the firing squad somewhere in Lincolnshire, 20 July 1944.

maintaining a limited service to be smuggled back into the country. Amongst these was the *Manchester Guardian* which, by a pre-war agreement, was kept in operation through the offices of *The Baltimore Sun* in America. Such contraband material brought severe penalties for those caught in its distribution, but for each copy in circulation the readership was enormous. Local papers carried on much as before, playing an increasingly important function as a centre of news and general information, though only a couple survived the paper famine of May 1944.

Radio in Britain was even more tightly controlled than the printed media. Two channels were set up: one was a German-language broadcast, mainly for the forces of occupation, the other a watered-down version of the BBC which consisted of German propaganda announcements mixed in with anodyne dance tunes and pieces of classical music. The selection policy excluded music by Jews (no Mendelssohn), Blacks (no jazz), other 'degenerates' and from June 1941, anything by Russian composers. A few BBC announcers were kept on, but after an incident when one brave man failed to keep to the script (he was sent to a death camp in Poland) all broadcasts were pre-recorded. Tuning into any other station was a punishable offence, although until the

setting up of the 'BBC Overseas' transmitters in North Africa and Spain (1944–5) few people in Britain were able to hear anything other than German-sponsored stations.

As the German authorities controlled the BBC and the newspapers with such an iron hand, so the resistance concentrated on building up an alternative news service. Attempts at clandestine local radio broadcasts failed (too limited a range and too easily located) so special news-sheets were prepared and distributed throughout Britain. The stories were reproduced from anti-Nazi sources, including the 'BBC Overseas'. These operations survived suppression, for whenever one 'printing works' was discovered and destroyed, another would open in its place. As well as providing a useful service to a population

Below The concentration camp outside Guildford during the main construction phase, spring-summer 1941. Although conditions were very harsh, the Guildford Camp was distinct from the death camps of Central and Eastern Europe, such as Auschwitz and Belsen.

starved of real news, the news-sheet distribution systems proved an effective means of building up sources of opposition.

The controversial documentary film *The Sorrow and the Pity* starkly revealed just how many British people collaborated with the Germans, a figure that came as a shock to post-war generations. At the end of the war, the collaborators shrank back into the shadows, while it seemed that almost the entire population had been active in the resistance – and it was this story of a dogged fight against a hated oppressor that became the new national mythology. The truth was that until 1945 the resistance never exceeded one or two per cent of the population; active collaboration reached its peak in 1943–4 with perhaps as many as two million people directly involved. The remainder somewhere in the middle – simply did their best to survive an increasingly desperate situation.

Something of the unique atmosphere of 'co-operation' is revealed by historian Norman Longmate, who quotes one man who survived a period as a hostage: 'People were a bit over-friendly, but in the circumstances it's hard to judge. There are people with stronger wills than others. The stronger wills were able to resist, the weaker wills gave way a little.' This charitable view of collaboration was not shared by all, as the hundreds of post-war 'Collaborator Trials' were to prove. But perhaps Longmate's source

had not seen the top British black market profiteers – the 'Reichsmark Millionaires' – dining at the luxurious Café Royal while their fellow countrymen starved, or seen those who had openly encouraged the arrest and deportation of the unfortunates given the 'one-way ticket'.

The British Union of Fascists (BUF) increased its membership enormously. Recruitment was concentrated on young thugs who actively supported the German authorities in their regular round-ups of 'undesirables'. Gangs roamed the streets of towns and cities, terrorizing any who appeared to oppose the New Order. Initially, Mosley gave qualified support to his own Blackshirt followers, but conflicts between his own-style 'patriotic fascism' and a new generation of young Nazi supporters saw him elbowed aside.

While the BUF bully-boys controlled the streets, collaboration at a higher level was conducted by

Below Cheering crowds of fascist supporters applaud a speaker at one of the Trafalgar Square meetings of the Anglo-German Union. Regular monthly fixtures, they developed into recruitment drives for the Legion of St George with the invasion of the Soviet Union.

Below Oswald Mosely gives the fascist salute in a celebration of his release from prison in the autumn of 1940. Mosely's 'patriotic fascism' proved unpopular with the new BUF leadership's pro-German 'United Europe' philosophy, and within a year he was formally expelled from the organization. His refusal to work directly with the Germans led to detention in the Tower with other VIP prisoners.

the Anglo-German Union (AGU), a revamp of the pre-war pro-Nazi organization, The Link. A number of businessmen and government officials found it expeditious to join the AGU – membership opened many useful doors to advancement. Some even argued that the New Order was not such a bad thing after all, acting as a bulwark against socialism and communism which kept the workers in their place. The AGU was officially encouraged by Goebbel's propaganda service, and well-publicized marches were a familiar sight during the first couple of years of occupation. The crackpot right-wing leadership of the AGU had high hopes for Britain to play a prominent role in Hitler's New Europe, but apart from a few publicity trips by AGU notables the organization had little or no influence on policy in Britain. This would always be kept securely in German hands.

While the average Briton's existence was a form of long, drawn-out purgatory, life for those groups and individuals selected by the Nazis for 'special treatment' was a living hell. Trade unions were banned and union leaders (regardless of their political convictions) were interned. The first institution to be raided by the Gestapo was the innocuous Brighton branch of the TGWU, the 'Special Search List' address given as (sic) '105 Ditschling Road'.

No one was surprised at the arrest of leading socialists, intellectuals and all those who had spoken out against appeasement in the 1930s. Most of those arrested knew their likely fate if captured. Some managed to get overseas – usually via the Republic of Ireland, until that route was closed – but others felt forced to take a more drastic form of escape – suicide.

Common to all those who took their own life was the belief that a swift death was preferable to the prolonged agony that capture by the Germans would entail. The famous left-wing publisher Victor Gollancz carried a lethal 'opium pill', to be taken on the point of seizure. The politician Harold Nicolson, also marked down by the Nazis, had made a suicide

Left An Irish smuggler meets a trawler from Fleetwood sailing with contraband cargo in the form of a dozen refugees fleeing from Nazi rule in the UK. This means of escape automatically ended with the German occupation of the Republic.

Above From the outset the German authorities attacked Britain's Jews, desecrating their synagogues (as with this one in Golders Green) and herding the population into ghettos.

pact with his wife as early as 26 May 1940, when he wrote: 'I am not in the least afraid of such [a] sudden and honourable death. What I dread is being tortured and humiliated.' Accurate suicide numbers are unavailable, but countless Gestapo torture-chamber victims must have envied such foresight and resolve.

Along with the random hostages taken as 'guarantees for good behaviour', the rough total of those arrested and interned during the first two years of the New Order (September 1940–December 1942) amounted to over 600,000 people. Almost half were Jews, the largest single target of Nazi hatred.

Most of the Jews were shipped over to the mainland, although some remained in Britain with non-Jewish internees in specially built camps, notably at Cumbernauld in Scotland, Oswestry in Shropshire and Guildford in Surrey. Sadly the British were not impermeable to the anti-semitism of the war years, and some Jews were sent to their deaths as a direct result of action by the indigenous population – perhaps the biggest scar on Britain's post-war conscience. On the other hand, several thousands of Jews were hidden by British gentiles, at great risk to themselves and their families. Inevitably, some of these were captured over the course of the occupation but others survived the ordeal.

Internment took diverse forms, reflecting the 'crimes' of the particular victim. They ranged from the death camps of Central Europe, through the holding camps in Britain to the special VIP quarters for specially favoured prisoners who were denied their liberty for the present but were considered as being potentially useful to the Nazis at some point in

Below Under police supervision Jews are directed onto waiting trains as part of a deportation order. The involvement of the British in the persecution of the Jews remains a controversial question. Besides the direct involvement of fascist and other anti-semitic groups, elements of Local Government, the Civil Service and the police all played their part in the shipment of Jews to the death camps.

the future. Most POWs had been shipped to Germany and set to work on the numerous construction projects intended to display to the world the glories of the Third Reich. A few, however, remained in Britain, housed in a dozen or so camps scattered across the country. The best known of these was the Little Wittenham (General Detention Camp) Berkshire, which housed senior British officers from the rank of Brigadier upwards. These former leaders of men were now employed in the construction of artificial limbs for the many casualties of the recent conflict.

For the great mass of people, the occupation was a grey period of monotonous struggle. Energies were concentrated on getting the bare essentials – fuel in winter and food all the time. A boy from a typically 'well-to-do' background gave the following account of life during the occupation:

'We lived in a large former rectory in Norfolk. My father, a major in the King's Own Yorkshire Light Infantry, had been deported to a POW camp in Silesia. That left the three of us – my mother, my younger brother and me. The housemaid, Ethel, also stayed on with us throughout the war. As we lived in a small rural town the first two or three years weren't so bad; we were able to get most things quite easily. A farmer friend kept us supplied with eggs for a while and by using every bit of the garden we built up a good potato store. But as time went by things got scarcer. My brother and I were always hungry. The supply of eggs dried up and with the end of coal rationing in 1943 we were forced to chop down everything in sight. My strongest memory is of us all sitting in the kitchen during the awful winter of 1944–5, huddled around a feeble fire (fuelled by the remains of my brother's rocking horse, not that he knew at the time) trying to keep warm as mother cooked a bit of meat – I've no idea what – for our Christmas lunch. It was the most miserable time of my life!'

The restrictions and rationing of the pre-invasion period had helped prepare people for material hardship, although as each year passed the situation worsened. Allotments became prized possessions and a successful vegetable gardener was someone to keep in with. Municipal and public parks were converted into market gardens, as were virtually all areas of cultivable ground, including (to the consternation of many) the pitches at Twickenham,

Wembly and Hampden, and even the grass tennis courts at Wimbledon. The most valued domestic lawns were dug up for vegetable patches. These measures all helped, but for a country which relied so heavily on the import of food, it was to prove insufficient.

When it became apparent that the Commonwealth and Empire nations refused to abide by the British surrender terms, openly supporting the Government-in-Exile instead, relations with these valuable sources of food supply ceased. America's entry into the war closed off Britain's other great food supplier. Trade with other countries – notably Argentina – was maintained for a short while but the majority of imports now came from Europe. Totally controlled by the Nazi economic system, the import of food became the major political issue between the British National Council and their German masters. The Germans repeatedly secured the acquiescence of the BNC by using two highly effective weapons: the threat of mass deportations and the control of food distribution. As the war progressed, so conditions worsened in Britain.

Left and <u>above</u> Food shortages became a chronic problem for the British population within months of the invasion, and got steadily worse as the years went by. In time, virtually all cultivable land was turned over to food production, including playing fields, public parks and – no matter how derelict – patches of city waste ground.

REPRESSION AND LIBERATION

The invasion of the Soviet Union in June 1941 brought Britain slowly but inexorably into the new European system. Industrial production was redirected to provide the German armed forces with munitions for the great war in the East. For a time during 1941 food rations were increased to stimulate productivity, although this did not last long. The spectacular advances made by the Germans in the first two years of fighting led a few thousand young Britons – mainly BUF supporters – to join the SS-sponsored Legion of St George in the 'Crusade against Bolshevism'. However, when the war began to turn against the Germans during 1944, recruitment fell off sharply.

Hitler's declaration of war against the United States of America early in 1942 had not been followed up by serious military action, both nations' attentions being focused on other theatres of war. But once the Japanese were in retreat in the Pacific, the US Joint Chiefs-of-Staff began to look to Europe. A combined Anglo-American Fleet crossed the Atlantic in March 1944 and battle-hardened US troops landed on North African soil without opposition from its Vichy French defenders. Throughout 1944 the Americans – with British, Commonwealth and Free French support –

established themselves in North Africa and the Iberian Peninsula. Meanwhile in the East, Soviet forces were slowly beginning to push the Germans out of the Russian heartland.

In 1945, the pace of the war increased. The strategic bombing offensive against German-occupied Europe began to take effect; Soviet forces reached their old pre-war borders with Poland; on 20 July an exhausted Japan surrendered. From then on, the entire weight of the American-Soviet armies concentrated on Germany which, despite falling back on all fronts, fought with the greatest skill and tenacity. On 15 September 1945, a combined US-Free Europe Force landed in the South of France in one of the most successful amphibious operations in the history of warfare. As the overstretched Germans began to fall back, the US President, Harry S. Truman, authorized the deployment of the weapon which would bring the Second World War to a close.

The momentous events of 1944–5 brought hope to the British people that liberation might be more than just a dream. They also brought vastly increased suffering, as the Nazi war economy brutally squeezed the country of all its resources in a frantic attempt to hold back the Allies. Although the twin German

Right President of the United States Harry S Truman meets King George VI aboard USS *Augusta* in Plymouth Harbor, shortly before the ship's voyage to European waters in August 1945. For five years the King and Government-in-Exile had been marooned thousands of miles from Britain; they awaited their return with equal measures of anticipation and trepidation.

Above Squadrons of USAAF B-24 heavy bombers attack the strategically vital Romanian oil refineries at Ploesti, October 1944. By early 1945 a decisive weight of US men and matériel had been deployed in the European Theater of Operations.

Left Even the Tower of London, domicile of the Nazi's VIP prisoners, did not escape the 'grow it at home' campaign.

disasters of Saratov and the Tula Hills in 1943 marked the turn of the tide in the European war, it was the invasion of North Africa early in 1944 which caused major German policy changes within Britain.

Churchill's historic 'end of the beginning' speech, broadcast on 1 May from Algiers to the people of Britain, led the German military authorities to abolish the British National Council and impose direct military rule. Sir Samuel Hoare, exhausted by the series of battles intended to moderate the more

Above British slave labourers work on a railway track repair operation, June 1944. By 1943 millions of European conscripted workers had been deported to the Reich to replace Germans for war service. Conditions were appalling, and many died of starvation and exhaustion.

rapacious German demands, found himself transported as yet another hostage to Germany. The Regent (Duke of Windsor) was also arrested 'for his own safety' and imprisoned with other VIP prisoners in the Tower of London. The parallel between Edward's fate and other royal forebears was further heightened by his death in captivity on 3 April 1945, from an alleged bout of bronchial pneumonia. Whether he died of natural causes or was murdered (by the Germans? the British?) remains a matter of debate, but the demise of this lonely and unpopular figure came as a relief to most everybody in Britain.

The Military Governor of Great Britain, General Gustav von Zanger, was replaced by the anti-partisan warfare specialist *SS Obergruppenführer* Erich von dem Bach-Zelewski, who took a far harder line than his predecessor. Transgressions of the criminal code were met with ever more severe punishments, and as resistance activity was re-established, so the taking and killing of hostages increased. And as Germany's demand for labour continued to grow, so the ever-threatened mass deportations of the male

population began in earnest. Any young man without a 'guarantee ticket' was liable for Reich Service. Units of the Army Occupation were used to round up enough men to meet monthly quotas from Berlin.

Few in Britain had any illusions about their likely treatment as a 'worker for Europe'; too many tales of slave-labour conditions had filtered back from Germany. While cattle-trucks full of deportees trundled towards the Channel ports, other potential victims went underground, helping swell the gangs of anti-German forces scattered across the country.

The winter of 1944–5 was a watershed of pov-

Above Large numbers of people had been driven from their homes during the occupation, and this trend increased dramatically in 1944 as a result of German punitive measures. Here, several families make their home in an ex-Salvation Army hostel in Manchester, December 1944.

erty. Food shipments from mainland Europe were stopped altogether. Allotments and dug-up gardens failed as a means of food supply for the large urban centres. Much of the produce from British farms still went straight to Germany – under strict guard. The spectre of starvation, which had hovered over the country for so long, now began to materialize. Malnutrition among the old and very young was evident; outbreaks of rickets and scurvy were so common they barely merited attention. During the harsh winter, thousands of deaths were directly attributable to food and fuel shortages. Coal from British mines was automatically exported overseas; wood, of any sort,

became the staple. Protests from tree-lovers were ignored in the desperate scramble for heat; tree-lined avenues were the first to go, followed in the course of time by whole forests.

Public utilities became equally scarce. Gas had always been in short and irritatingly irregular supply; electricity had been reasonably constant until the end of 1944 when one or two hours a day became the norm. Water, by contrast, was maintained until the end – partly because it was not a major drain on essential resources but also because of the German Army's strict injunctions against the prevention of infectious diseases through poor sanitation.

The inevitable corollary of increased shortages was rapid inflation, especially on the black market, following the breakdown of rationing in the spring of 1945. Motor vehicles – except those required for official German business – were a relic of the past. Bicycles were the only form of transport for most people, and prices were astronomical. A basic model costing around £5 in pre-war days had shot up to 10 times that amount by the end of 1944. Clothes, footwear, tobacco and, of course, food fetched the highest prices. Everyday household objects started being priced in guineas, becoming 'luxury articles'. In April 1945 a pair of reconditioned boots might cost 12 guineas (£12.60p); a pound of butter retailed at three guineas (£3.15p); a packet of 20 (Turkish) cigarettes two guineas (£2.10p) and a single egg would go for as much as 10s 6d (52½p). Regardless of price, the supply of goods often dried up altogether; more than ever, knowing the right people made all the difference.

Everyone who endured the last phase of the occupation had his or her tale of deprivation: making do with 'nettle brew' when tea rations gave out; being served watery stews where politeness (and fear of what the answer may be) dictated that no one enquire of the meat's origin; smoking lethal home-grown tobacco; and especially, the hours spent queueing for goods which inevitably ran out just as you reached the counter. And yet the people of Britain and Western Europe survived better than those of Central and Eastern Europe, who were subjected to the full force of the Nazis' psychopathic ideology.

The dormant phase of British resistance ended with the North African landings. The formal Allied commitment to the invasion and liberation of Europe (the Casablanca Conference of 1944) gave more than hope to the various opposition movements. At last, plans were made to provide the organizations with money, weapons and equipment. Above all, a framework for a co-ordinated plan of opposition to German rule was drawn up. France was justifiably given top priority, and although Britain had become something of an outpost in the German Empire, its resistance movements received a good share of the available resources.

The popular idea of a homogenized resistance movement in every occupied country was something of a myth. All these movements comprised a collection of groups whose essential and sometimes sole unifying bond was a determination to be rid of the invader. In Britain the first and main focus of armed opposition came from ex-servicemen, although other significant groups included communists based in the larger towns and cities and various nationalist organizations in Wales, Scotland and, especially, Ireland.

The main function of the Anglo-American SOE/ OSS teams, secretly smuggled into the country, was to co-ordinate operations and cause the Germans maximum damage. Supplies of radio sets, weapons and explosives enabled active operations to be resumed during the summer of 1944. Although it was clear that the United Kingdom would not be an important combat zone, the Germans would never be prepared to relinquish such a prize without a fight. The resistance could take justifiable satisfaction in the large numbers of German forces stationed in Britain and Ireland (over 400,000 in November 1944), many tied down in anti-partisan activities.

Just by looking at the map it was fairly clear that England did not lend itself to the classic partisan operations carried out by the resistance movements in Yugoslavia and the Soviet Union. Wales and Scotland became the main battlegrounds for this new form of warfare. A small band of freedom fighters would ambush an enemy convoy and slip back miles into the mountains before any sort of concerted German action could be organized to catch them. Of

Above A British civilian pours carefully hoarded petrol into his car. The original caption claims he is a 'doctor'; his 'occupation' is more likely that of black marketeer or German agent.

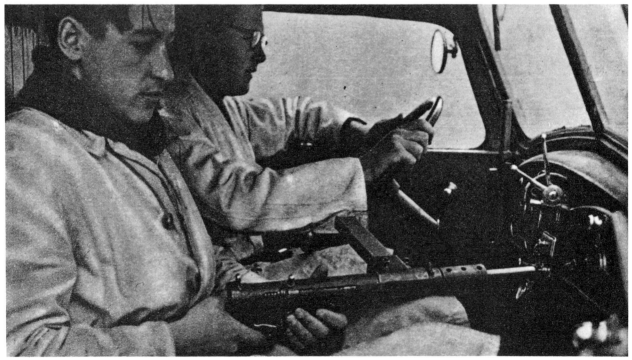

Top A picture often captioned as an attack on a regional Gestapo HQ, but the fact that the man on the right wields a Tommy gun without a magazine suggests it as mere photo-propaganda.

Above A resistance team poses for the camera before setting out on a mission. The weapon is a 'Sten' sub-machine gun, manufactured in Canada especially for use by the resistance.

Above German troops move up along a wooded valley in Ullswater as part of the operation to destroy the Lakeland Uprising. No matter how capable the resistance was, it could never take on the Wehrmacht in conventional actions. Naively the British thought the mountains of Westmoreland and Cumberland would act to their advantage, little realising the depth of German experience in anti-partisan operations in the Balkans.

Right Lord Lovat, leader of the Rob Roy Commando, photographed after a particularly hard mission against the German garrison holding Fort William, 19 August 1944. Of all the various resistance groups active during the occupation this was the most effective, owing its success to the difficult Scottish terrain and the fighting skills of its members.

course, the local communities suffered terribly. In certain parts of North Wales and the Scottish Highlands, whole villages were destroyed by enemy reprisals, or abandoned by their inhabitants who fled into the hills. In these areas, the occupation took on a new and bitter form, largely unknown in southern England.

In North Wales, a resistance band calling itself the 'Brothers of Owen Glendower' scored a number of spectacular successes against the Germans, who occasionally found themselves virtually besieged in the garrisons of Caernarvon and Rhyl. In Scotland, the Highland resistance centred around the activities of the Commandos, who had been in active opposition ever since the summer of 1940. Known as the Rob Roy Commando, their exploits were causing the Germans such problems that Hitler personally ordered the transfer of the notorious SS *Prinz Eugen* Mountain Division from anti-partisan duties in the Balkans. The arrival of this formation in Scotland in November 1944 was largely counter-production; despite the atrocities it carried out, the local population refused to be broken and instead their activities produced a surge of recruitment for the Scottish resistance.

In Ireland, the Germans had hoped to exploit the religious and political complexities of the country to their advantage, but this approach did not succeed. Clumsy attempts to operate a divide-and-rule system between Protestants and Catholics failed miserably. As staunch Loyalists, the Protestants would have no dealings with the Germans on principle, and most Catholics regarded the Germans with deepest contempt. The small German garrison in Ireland was eventually reinforced to army corps level as a vicious guerrilla warfare developed.

The standard German system of control by reprisal did not work in the Republic. Every hostage shot merely produced a martyr to be avenged; every sacking of a village evoked violent folk memories of Cromwell and Drogheda. Having just gained their independence from one long occupation, the Irish were not prepared to accept another.

Once people realized that Germany would eventually lose the war, their sense of hopelessness was replaced by an increasingly strong desire to be involved in the final expulsion. In England communist and socialist groups had done valuable work in reducing the output of German war goods; vital machinery mysteriously broke down; rolling stock was constantly being derailed; coal production tar-

gets were never met. In addition, small-scale raids against military targets recommenced in the summer of 1944, along with well-publicized assassinations of leading collaborators and black market profiteers – object lessons to all whose dealings with the Germans exceeded what one resistance leader termed 'the dictates of necessity'. The Germans dealt with these activities with traditional severity. The scent of victory, however, gave the British renewed courage and optimism and despite horrific reprisals, guerrilla activity increased right up until the liberation.

One notable resistance failure was the attempt to set up an 'independent zone' in the English Lake District in September 1945 – a grave tactical error inspired by enthusiasm for the successful invasion in France. The Germans reacted with the greatest resolve. Selected units from the two mountain divisions stationed in Britain were joined by the SS Parachute Battalion and the 21st Panzer Division – recovering from its recent mauling on the Eastern Front. The 3,000-strong alliance of partisan groups that had declared an 'Independent Lakeland' on 25 September stood no chance as the Germans set about systematically destroying the main towns of Keswick and Windermere before sending its sweep and cordon missions into the mountains to isolate and destroy the British. Less than 250 guerrillas slipped through the German net before the officer in charge of the operation telexed OKW with the news that the area was 'cleansed of all bandits'.

The resistance in Britain can be counted as a success in that it helped distract a number of German troops who otherwise would have been deployed on the main fronts, and also because it returned a sense of pride to a nation that had been devastated by its failures on the battlefields of 1940. One thing the resistance could not do, however, was liberate the country on its own. The disaster in the Lake District proved beyond doubt that guerrilla forces could not survive in open warfare against a determined opponent. Britain would have to await the arrival of direct outside help.

The speed of the Allied advance from its beachheads in southern France caught the Germans by surprise. Short of men and equipment, Field Marshal von Rundstedt (Supreme Commander West) ignored Hitler's orders to stand fast and conducted a skilful retreat through France to the Ludendorff Line, a defensive system running from the Swiss border across northern France to Le Havre on the Channel Coast. By early December the Germans took up their new positions with the Allied armies in hot pursuit. Salvation for Britain was now close at hand, although strong German forces remained in Britain as Bach-Zelewski obeyed Hitler's injunction to stand firm. Throughout November and December, squadrons of the RAF and USAAF flew over Britain, attacking key strong points and alerting the population to the fact that help was finally on its way.

Despite Churchill's repeated requests for an invasion force to be launched across the Channel, the Allied Supreme Command insisted that first priority was the defeat of the German Army in the field. This meant a long campaign which would carry the war over at least until the summer of 1946. Fortunately for the people of Britain, who faced another winter of starvation, outside events dramatically forced the pace of the campaign.

On 12 December a large force of US bombers set off to attack Hamburg in what was assumed to be another follow-up raid to the missions of early November. Amidst the biggest fighter escort of the war, however, was a B-29 which was carrying an atomic bomb. The bomb was dropped right on target and the city was flattened. A similar operation was launched against Nuremburg two days later, with even more devastating results. The German High Command was stunned. Rumours of the terrible destruction wrought by these bombs spread across Germany. This was a new terror weapon, against which the Führer's much-vaunted V-2 rocket paled into insignificance.

Hitler was showing increasing signs of dementia, and plots to overthrow him, especially after the So-viet occupation of East Prussia in October 1945, were already current. The devastation caused by the atomic bombs called for urgent action. On 20 December Hitler, with Bormann, Himmler and Goebbels, was arrested by Army officers. All four were shot the following day after a summary trial.

Chaos broke out in Germany as troops loyal to Hitler fought it out with units under the command of the December Coup leaders. But the outcome was never in doubt: a few fanatical Nazis (mainly Hitler Youth members) refused to give up but most Germans were only too keen to end the hopeless struggle. Germany had lost the war and its new leaders knew it. On 25 December 1945 German forces surrendered unconditionally to the Allies. As one wit remarked: 'At least the war was over *on* Christmas.'

For the people of Britain, the arrival of troops of the 2nd British (Free) Division at Dover on 26 December was a perfect Christmas present. The following day the battleship *Duke of York* manoeuvred slowly into the docks at Southampton. An enormous crowd watched King George VI, followed by his Prime Minister, walk down the gangplank on to English soil once more.

Above The triumph of liberation: British paratroopers are welcomed by the people of a small fishing village, one of the lead elements of the 2nd British (Free) Division, 26 December 1945. The German armed forces officially surrendered the next day; the war was over.

BIBLIOGRAPHICAL NOTE

In the five decades since the invasion of Great Britain, there has been a steady flow of histories on the subject. I have relied heavily on the following works which cover the specific aspects of the conflict. Ronald Wheatley's *Operation Sea Lion* (Oxford, 1958) and Walter Ansel's *Hitler Confronts England* (Duke University Press, 1960) deal extensively with German preparations. Peter Schenk's *Landing in England* (Oberbaum Verlag GmbH, 1987) is a detailed examination of the amphibious aspects of the assault. On the other side of the Channel, Basil Collier's *The Defence of the United Kingdom* (HMSO, 1957) forms part of the British Official History of the Second World War. Peter Fleming's *Invasion 1940* (Rupert Hart-Davies, 1957) was written by the Auxiliary Officer responsible for Kent but deals with the whole British response to the invasion. Norman Longmate's *If Britain had Fallen* (BBC/Hutchinson, 1972) considers both the preparations and the invasion itself and then goes on to examine life in Britain under the Nazi jackboot with great thoroughness. David Lampe's *The Last Ditch* (Cassell, 1968) is an informative study of the setting up of resistance networks in Britain and German intentions for the running of the country, Lastly, Kenneth Macksey's *Invasion: The German Invasion of England, July 1940* (Arms and Armour Press, 1980) is a comprehensive history of the whole campaign up to the British surrender, covering both British and German viewpoints with considerable impartiality.

Two of the more important German documents relating to the occupation were published in Leipzig in 1941 and reprinted as facsimiles in the 1960s. They are: *Orders concerning Organisation and Function of Military Government in England* and *German Occupied Britain: Ordinances of the Military Authorities* (both Scutt-Dand, Foord, 1967). When the full extent of the names included in the SS *Sonderfahndungsliste GB* was realised after the war, it became something of a matter of pride to have been included, and copies held by the Imperial War Museum were avidly consulted. In 1989 the IWM published a facsimile copy of the book. Hitler's 'Sealion Directive No. 16: On preparations for a landing operation against England' can be found in *Hitler's War Directives*, edited by Hugh Trevor-Roper (Sidgwick and Jackson, 1964).

Alister Horne's *To Lose a Battle: France 1940* (Macmillan, 1969) explains how and why the Allies failed in France, while Len Deighton's *Blitzkrieg* (Jonathan Cape, 1979) demonstrates the reasons for German success. *Fighter: The True Story of the Battle of Britain* (Cape, 1977) also by Deighton and F. K. Mason's *Battle Over Britain* (McWhirter, 1969) cover the aerial prelude to invasion. On intelligence matters, Richard Deacon's *The Greatest Treason* (Century, 1989) confirms what was widely held as rumour and R. G. Grant's *MI5/MI6* (Bison, 1989) provides a sound and well illustrated overview. On the Duke of Windsor's role in the war there is the SD chief's own if less than totally reliable account – Walther Schellenberg's *The Schellenberg Memoirs* (Andre Deutsch, 1956) – and Peter Allen's *The Crown and the Swastika* (Robert Hale, 1983), a study of the ex-monarch during this period. For a modern overview of the war there is John Keegan's *The Second World War* (Hutchinson, 1989) and Martin Gilbert's *Second World War* (Weidenfeld and Nicolson, 1989).

An event of this magnitude has produced its own fictional literature, some of it of considerable interest to historians of the period. Prominent amongst these are *Loss of Eden* by Douglas Brown and Christopher Serpell (Faber, 1940) and the more recent *SS-GB* by Len Deighton (Cape, 1978) – both concerned with life during the occupation. The naval author C. S. Forester wrote two short stories of the invasion, which are to be found in a posthumous collection, published as *Gold From Crete* (Michael Joseph, 1971).

INDEX

Page numbers in *italics* refer to picture captions

Picture acknowledgements

Photographs for this book were supplied by the Imperial War Museum, Library of Congress, Robert Hunt Picture Library, Tom Rippley Associates, US Army, US Air Force, US National Archive.
The Department of Photographs at the Imperial War Museum, Lambeth Road, London SE1 6HZ has a visitor's room which is open to the public by appointment. The Museum has an extensive collection of World War I and World War II photographs, many available for purchase.